Finding
LOVE
In
RECOVERY

Finding LOVE *In* RECOVERY

By
Terence T. Gorski
and
Bonnie S. Zannini

Based on the CENAPS Model of Relationship Health

Herald House / Independence Press
Independence, Missouri

Independence, Missouri

Additional copies of this book and other addictions resources based on the CENAPS Model of Treatment can be obtained through the publisher:

Herald House/Independence Press
3225 South Noland Road
P.O. Box 1770
Independence, MO 64055-0770
Telephone: 1-800-767-8181 or 816/252-5010
Fax: 816/252-3976
Internet Web Page: http://www.heraldhouse.org
E-mail: hhmark@heraldhouse.org

Library of Congress Cataloging-in-Publication Data
    Gorski, Terence T.
    Finding love in recovery / by Terence T. Gorski and Bonnie S. Zannini.
        p.   cm.
    ISBN 0-8309-0773-4
    1. Narcotic addicts—Rehabilitation. 2. Alcoholics—Rehabilitation. 3. Single people—Drug use. 4. Single people—Alcohol use. 5. Interpersonal conflict. 6. Codependency.
I. Zannini, Bonnie S.   II. Title.
HV5801.G67   1997   97-7829
362.29'18—dc21   CIP

01 00 99 98 97   1 2 3 4 5

This book is dedicated to:

Carmela
and
Ron
For the love we found...

Table of Contents

Single and in Recovery:
The Overlooked Population

The first time Jake gave a lead at his regular Sunday night AA step meeting, he talked a little bit about some of the problems he'd been having with relationships—finding them, losing them, getting into them, staying out of them, doing without them, and communicating about them. The topic seemed appropriate: It was a first-step meeting—about powerlessness and the unmanageability of his life—and he felt as if he had reached rock-bottom on the problems of being single in recovery. But he was also a little afraid to talk about it. He was only one year sober, and some of the people at the meeting had ten or more years' recovery. Wouldn't they think it was stupid and dangerous to be even thinking about relationships at this stage of recovery, much less talking about them in a lead?

> **In this chapter, you'll look at:**
> - Challenges that singles in recovery often face
> - Special challenges for women and men
> - Special challenges for gay men and lesbians
> - Hope for singles in recovery

When he heard the other members' comments, Jake was surprised. Almost everyone in the room was struggling, in one way or another, with conflicts and confusion related to being single.

Val was in the middle of a messy divorce, fighting for custody of her two sons. Maria had gone into a depression after her husband died seven years ago; since then she'd been avoiding relationships but feeling empty inside. Lemont was struggling with the question of whether it would be fair to ask his girlfriend to marry him while he was still working two jobs to pay alimony and child support. Joyce had recently relapsed after she stopped going to her regular meetings, trying to avoid running into a man she'd been involved with. After many sober relationships, Rob was still finding that his new partner brought up all the unhealed anger from his childhood. And Jana was staying out of relationships for a while in order to work on herself, but it hurt when some of her friends stopped inviting her out because she didn't have a partner.

Jake couldn't believe it. Some of these people seemed to have everything going for them. They were smart, attractive, successful, and working solid recovery programs. Why did this area of their lives cost them so much pain, upset, work, and worry?

Being single and sober is hard. Facing the pain and problems in life—without the alcohol and drugs that once seemed to take away the pain—can be difficult at any stage of recovery. In or out of relationships, people who have been divorced, widowed, or never married have their own special kinds of problems. If you add to those problems the challenge of learning to live a clean and sober life, then you need special help. Trying to do without that help can lead to unhappiness, depression, or even relapse. Many, many people are grieving friends and family members who relapsed over these kinds of issues and never made it back into recovery. The sad irony is that the chemicals they took to escape the pain of facing life created much greater pain, for them and for those who cared about them.

Many sponsors and others in self-help groups will tell you to "work the steps" (the Twelve Steps of Alcoholics Anonymous) on the problems of being single, but what exactly does that mean? If you feel empty when you're not in a relationship—and feel crazy when you are—you need something much more concrete and specific. First you need to look at the effects of addiction on your past relationships, and on your way of operating in or out of relationships. Then you need to look at where you are in your recovery process, and the special relationship-related problems and tasks you face at this stage of recovery. Finally, you need to build skills that will help you avoid falling into the old traps, and you need a plan that will help you build the kind of life and relationships that will support your recovery and your long-term happiness. This book will walk you through those processes, and show you how they relate to 12-Step principles. It will show you that, even though you're single, you're definitely not alone.

> *Facing the pain and problems in life and*
> *relationships—without the alcohol and drugs*
> *that once seemed to take away the pain—can*
> *be difficult at any stage of recovery.*

First, a quick definition of the word "single." As it's used in this book, this word refers to people who are not presently in a committed romantic partnership. Many years ago, most committed romantic partnerships were called "marriage" and were licensed and recorded. Now many people have committed partnerships that are just as strong as any marriage, but they're not registered as legal arrangements. Some of these partnerships are celebrated with a ceremony in which vows are exchanged; others are not. The authors consider people's commitment to these partnerships every bit as binding as the commitment to marriage. They are not included in the category "single." Many people who are single have relationships. These relationships might last a long time or a short time. But if both partners haven't made that solemn commitment to stay together in partnership, they're considered single for the purposes of this book.

Every so often as you're reading this book, you'll find a series of "Thought and Discussion Questions." Answering these questions as honestly as you can will make your experience of the book much more rewarding. There are several ways you can do this: You can think about your answers; you can write them in your journal (or start a special journal for this purpose); and/ or you can talk about them with a friend, your recovery group sponsor, your therapist, or a group of single and sober people.

You'll also notice a number of references to one or more of the steps used in 12-Step recovery groups like Alcoholics Anonymous, Narcotics Anonymous, Cocaine Anonymous, Al-Anon, etc. We realize that, while many readers may be involved in 12-Step recovery, not all will be members of these groups or familiar with the steps. So the steps are listed and explained briefly in the appendix that begins on page197.

> *With all the deep and committed friendships available to you in recovery, you don't ever have to go back to the kind of loneliness you felt in active addiction.*

The Challenges

Let's take a look at some of the challenges that singles in recovery often face. These challenges are divided into three groups: Attitudes toward being single, getting used to being single and sober, and feelings that can trigger relapse. One important note: The word "relationship" can mean any kind of relationship—family, business, friendship, etc. But most of the time when we use it in this book, it refers to dating, romantic, or sexual relationships.

Attitudes Toward Being Single

It's normal to have conflicting feelings about being single. More and more adults in our society are spending more time before or between marriages or other "official" relationships. For example, 61 percent of the population in urban America is single (divorced, widowed, or never married). There isn't as much open shame or fear connected with being single as there used to be, but some of the old shame and fears have simply "gone underground." Many people who appear happy and confident with their single lifestyle are really struggling with self-doubt. They ask themselves the three core questions of being single:

1. If I'm single, will I always be alone?
2. What do I have to offer to others as a single person?
3. If I'm single, am I unlovable or undesirable?

These questions are hard for anyone to tackle. But for people whose lives and relationships have been torn apart by the effects of addiction, the questions are even harder. Their answers take on all the fears that the addictive past created. Substance abuse often comes out of—and leads to—isolation, low self-esteem, and feelings of being unlovable. Hopelessness is the name of the game. And when people reach recovery, just because the substances are taken away, it doesn't mean that hope will magically appear. Hope has to be built, slowly, with help from other people.

But what does hope mean for you? With a history of self-destructive life patterns, you might be missing some information about who you are and what would really make you happy in the long run. It will take time in recovery—alone and in relationships—to discover the full truth about yourself. For some people, being single is a life stage, a time to grow and develop before settling into a committed relationship. For others, it's a lifestyle, a preferred way of living. Not everyone wants to be in a long-term committed relationship, and not everyone should be.

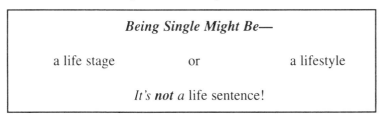

Being Single Might Be—

a life stage   or   a lifestyle

*It's **not** a life sentence!*

Later in this book you'll have a chance to look more closely at what being single means in your life. In the meantime, it's important to remember that a single woman or man is a complete person. The more complete you make your life as a single person, the happier you'll be and the more you'll bring into every human relationship. With all the deep and committed friendships available to you in recovery, you don't ever have to go back to the kind of loneliness you felt in active addiction.

Whether being single is a life stage or a lifestyle, it's a mistake to think of it as a "life sentence," a state you're doomed to stay in because of your real or imagined imperfections. If you haven't felt successful so far in relationships, it doesn't mean you're bad or "defective." You've probably made what we call "selection errors": choosing partners who don't work out for you in the long run. You may also have some issues of your own to work through before your relationships will succeed, no matter who your partners are. This book will help you identify and start to work on those issues. You can also look for help in a singles recovery group.

Thought and Discussion Questions

1. When you hear someone described as a "single man" or a "single woman," what's your first thought about that person?
2. Do you think of being single as a life stage, a lifestyle, or a life sentence? Please explain.
3. When you're alone for a period of time, how do you feel? What do you do?
4. What is the best thing about being single and sober? What is the worst thing?

Getting Used to Being Single and Sober

People who use alcohol and drugs addictively have a set of unwritten rules that are very different from those in the recovering world. Many people find it hard to get used to the change.

For example, in the using world, you could escape the fear of rejection and the fear of being truly close to someone. All you had to do was hide behind the mask of alcohol or drugs. In sobriety, you're out in the open, and so is the other person. You meet people sober, you go out for coffee sober, you even go to dances sober. If you get involved, you go out on dates sober, and whatever else happens—you get the idea. This is scary until you get used to it.

In the addictive world, it's not just alcohol and drugs that get used. People get used too. Some people are used for sex, and others are used to get alcohol or drugs. In social situations, people are often expected to get sexually involved. Otherwise they get the message that they're wasting their partner's time. In recovery, the ideal is much different. People are there to help one another get sober and stay sober. If they're attracted to one another, that has to take a back seat to the first goal: mutual sobriety. That ideal isn't always honored, but you can find and stick to groups and friends who do keep sobriety first. That way you can stay safe and learn to relate simply as human beings. Your sobriety will be stronger if you do, and your relationships will be stronger, too—when you're ready for them.

Thought and Discussion Questions

1. How did you use your addiction to cope with social situations?
2. What part of sober social life is the most challenging or frightening to you?
3. What do you do to stay emotionally safe in social situations?

Feelings that Can Trigger Relapse

If you're single in recovery—especially in early recovery—you may be experiencing special problems. Even as your body is getting used to living without alcohol or drugs, your mind is probably starting to look for new things to be dependent on, new addictions to distract you from the pain and frustration of life. You may feel an emptiness where the alcohol and drugs used to go. In a society whose movie, television, and popular music industries are all focused on romantic love as the answer to all your questions and the cure for all your ills, it's easy to interpret that emptiness as the need for love or sex. The desire to get involved with someone can be overwhelming.

Sooner or later, you might find yourself feeling infatuated with someone—that first stage of involvement where you see only the attractive side of the other person, and he or she raises very strong sexual and romantic feelings in you. You might find the feelings of infatuation overwhelming and hard to handle but so pleasant that you keep wanting more. Infatuation works like an addictive substance. It releases chemicals in your brain that give you pleasure and take you out of the pain, boredom, and frustration of your everyday life.

Infatuation:

- works like an addictive substance
- can bring you back to an addictive way of dealing with the world
- uses a person instead of a drink or a drug

This is dangerous because it brings you back to that addictive way of dealing with the world. Your "addictive self" says, "If life is unpleasant, use something outside yourself to distract you, to take your unpleasant feelings away, and to replace them with good feelings." The only difference is that this time you're using a person instead of a drink or a drug. But it reawakens that part of you that's used to looking for a "fix." Once that part is awakened, it can trigger strong cravings for the substances you used to control your moods. Add to this the possibility that you don't know how to have a good time in social situations without those substances and you have a very dangerous situation.

The most dangerous situation of all is getting or staying involved with someone who still drinks or uses, or someone whose sobriety is shaky. This might be someone you knew before you entered recovery. You might tell yourself that, with your love and your positive example, your partner might also find recovery. But you know from your own experience that people can keep using for a long time, no matter how much love and how many good examples they have. People who stay in relationships with active addicts often have a hard time getting sober. The sight and smell of the substances, and seeing people get high, can trigger strong urges and cravings. Their chances at successful recovery are much lower than they would be if they broke off those relationships. In many cases it comes down to a choice between your relationship and your life.

Thought and Discussion Questions

1. Have you ever been tempted to relapse, or actually relapsed, when you were feeling infatuated with someone?
2. If you're in a relationship with an active alcoholic or addict, why are you staying in that relationship right now?

Special Challenges for Women and Men

All people are created equal, but we often have different ways of coping with life and relating to one another. Along with the challenges of being single and sober, you probably have special challenges related to being a woman or being a man. If you're gay or lesbian, you also may have some extra stress to contend with. You'd be cheating yourself not to look at how your gender and sexual preference might be affecting your feelings about yourself and your relationships in sobriety.

When we talk about the different issues that affect men and women, we're often talking about opposite sides of the same coin. Many women have been encouraged all their lives to develop and use the "softer," more passive sides of their nature as human beings. In recovery, we sometimes call this the "codependent" side. A codependent style is a way of coping that involves giving in, pleasing others, taking care of their problems, and not showing your own strength. Sometimes this is called a **Type-B Personality**.

Many men have been encouraged to develop their "tough," aggressive sides. We sometimes call this the "counterdependent" side. The counterdependent style is a way of coping by winning, taking power and control, and not showing weakness—except temporarily, when it would help you gain control. Sometimes this is called a **Type-A Personality**.

Each gender contains the full range of human possibilities, but we wear certain personality traits on the outside, while we keep others hidden inside. Sometimes we even hide those traits from ourselves. If we live too far toward one end of the scale or the other—too tough or too soft—our lives are unbalanced. We aren't able to admit and cope with the emotions that belong to the hidden "shadow side" of ourselves, and there are many healthy behaviors that we don't allow ourselves to consider. One of the tasks of recovery is to find and develop that shadow side, so that we can lead more balanced lives. So, for example, in recovery you'll see many tough, counterdependent people allowing themselves to feel their softer emotions for the first time, and many codependent people practicing being more assertive.

Where do you think you are on this scale?
(Circle one number.)

Codependency/Counterdependency Scale		
Codependent	**Balanced**	**Counterdependent**
10 9 8 7 6 5 4	3 2 1 0 1 2 3	4 5 6 7 8 9 10
I must be compliant and pleasing.	I'm comfortable with my strength and	I must be strong and demanding.
I can't assert my strength.	my weakness.	I can't show any weakness.

People with codependent styles tend to attract people with counterdependent styles, and vice versa. People whose personalities are balanced (within the zero-to-three range in the scale above) tend to attract other balanced people. The farther toward one end of the scale you are, the more extreme the partners you'll tend to attract.

Thought and Discussion Questions

1. If you're closer to the codependent or counterdependent end of the scale, how does this tendency come out in your relationships?
2. Does this cause any problems in your relationships? Please explain.

Single, Sober, and Female

There is no "typical" woman, but there are many issues that are more common to women than to men, or tend to cause more discomfort for them. For example, our society tends to think of chemical dependency as much more shameful in a woman than in a man. This is a holdover of the old myths that saw addiction as a sign of weak will or weak character. Women who were addicted were thought to be unfit wives or mothers, and sexually "easy."

Issues that many single, sober women face:

- The stereotype of the chemically dependent woman
- The superwoman syndrome
- The stress of being the custodial parent
- Issues of sexual victimization
- Abandonment issues

The Stereotype of the Chemically Dependent Woman. Medical science has proved the old myths about addiction false. Unfortunately, though, many people are superstitious and slow to grasp new information, especially if it challenges the beliefs that they were handed down as children. Within recovery programs, the term "recovering alcoholic or addicted woman" calls up images of strong, successful women. But outside the program, people often don't know about the strength that can come to people in recovery. They just see the old stereotype of the alcoholic woman. This prejudice can lead some women to doubt themselves in social situations and cause big problems for divorcing women who want custody of their children.

The Stress of Being the Custodial Parent. If you've ever raised children alone, you know how incredibly stressful that can be. More women than men become custodial parents after divorce, and many women who have babies without being married automatically take on full responsibility for their children. There's tremendous financial stress, emotional stress, and the added stress of having no partner to share the burden of child care, transportation, etc. For many women, motherhood itself can be confusing. The old myths about mothers tell us that women naturally and automatically love their children and want to be mothers. That's not always true, though. Many good women, and good mothers, have mixed feelings about their roles and about their children. Not knowing that this confusion is normal, they feel guilty about it. These kinds of burdens can put extra strain on a woman's recovery program and on her relationships.

Unhealed emotional wounds from sexual victimization can make recovery more painful and make it hard to build trust in new relationships.

The Superwoman Syndrome. One issue that a number of women face is the belief that they need to "do it all"—career, marriage, children, social life, and taking care of their parents as they grow older. Sometimes the many roles conflict with one another, and the woman questions who she is, what she wants, and what's important to her on the deepest levels. But at that point she feels locked into her obligations on all fronts. This can lead to feelings of being trapped, used, and misunderstood. Because no one can be perfect in all those areas, she can also have strong feelings of failure. Her recovery program can go on the "back burner" as she scurries around trying to be everything to everyone.

Issues of Sexual Victimization. Another common problem that many women face is the possibility or the reality of being sexually victimized, in or out of relationships. Most women who report having been raped were raped by men they knew, and researchers estimate that large numbers of "date rapes" are never reported. Even more women are talked into having sex although they're not ready to or don't really want to. Unhealed emotional wounds from sexual victimization can make recovery more painful, and can make it hard to build trust in new relationships.

There's also the danger of sexual victimization in recovery. In the using world, where sex is often used as "payment" for drugs or a night on the town, women are often expected to have sex if their partner wants it. Some people bring those attitudes with them into recovery, and present a hidden danger in an environment where women are supposed to be safe.

Issues of Abandonment. One very painful issue for many women is the fear of being abandoned. An adult can't really be abandoned like a child can, because an adult isn't helpless, even though it sometimes might feel that way. But an adult can lose an important relationship—through death, divorce, etc.—and it can trigger old fears and feelings of abandonment that are left over from childhood. Along with the full load of recovery issues, many women also struggle with those old fears and feelings. When abandonment issues are at the forefront, being single can feel like being all alone.

Fear of abandonment is also a major factor leading many women to stay in relationships with partners who are still active in their chemical dependency. If they're in recovery, these women know the danger of remaining involved with their partners. But those childhood fears of abandonment are so strong that the idea of leaving the relationship seems more dangerous than staying. Men are more likely to leave an addicted partner than women are. Women tend to stay with actively addicted partners. The fear of abandonment may have a lot to do with that tendency.

Many women who have been widowed tend to feel as if they've been abandoned by the death of their husbands. Many divorced women also feel abandoned. If there are children, the abandonment feelings can be intensified. The stresses and responsibilities are greater, leading to stronger feelings of helplessness and hopelessness.

Denise had almost a year in recovery when her husband died of lung cancer. At that point she faced serious financial trouble and felt as if her program was simply "unraveling." She felt abandoned by her husband, by his doctors, and by her attorney, who was a friend of her husband's and had promised to take care of her and her four children. Finally she started talking to friends in her NA meeting about how she was feeling, and one of them put her in touch with a therapist who could help her through the grieving process. Through that therapist she started participating in a grief support group. With all those forms of support on her side, Denise made it through the most difficult months of the grieving process.

Women tend to stay with actively addicted partners, whereas men tend to leave. The fear of abandonment may have a lot to do with that tendency.

Fears and feelings of abandonment that have their roots in childhood can make the normal emotions of grieving even more difficult. For people in recovery, this can easily raise the risk of relapse. Fear of abandonment can also make it hard to form new relationships when it's time to start again. And when people do start new relationships, strong fears of abandonment can sabotage the relationships and actually drive their partners away.

Thought and Discussion Questions

1. If you're a woman, have you ever run into problems with the stereotypical image of the alcoholic or addicted woman? What were those problems?
2. Are you a single, custodial parent? What kinds of problems has that role caused in your life, your sobriety, and/ or your relationships?
3. Have you ever experienced the superwoman syndrome? What kinds of problems has that caused in your life, your sobriety, and/or your relationships?
4. Have you ever been victimized sexually or physically by past or current partners? How have those experiences affected your life, your sobriety, and/or your relationships?
5. Have you ever experienced fear of abandonment? How have those fears affected your life, your sobriety, and/or your relationships?

Single, Sober, and Male

Like women, men also have special challenges in recovery. For many men, alcohol and other drugs weren't their only armor against uncomfortable emotions. They had a whole society teaching them that they didn't feel what they felt, that they were too "tough" to feel pain. When the substances are removed in recovery, and men are taught that emotional honesty is necessary for their survival, many feel defenseless—and sometimes defensive. Here are a few of the challenges that many men face.

Roles and Stereotypes of Men. For the past several decades much attention has been focused on the need to reexamine and redefine women's roles in our society. It's only much more lately that any attention has fallen on the need to look at men's roles, and that attention hasn't been anywhere near as widespread. For many men, the old stereotypical male roles don't work anymore. They don't want to be super tough heroes, or glamour boys, or any of the rest of those images. They just want to be who they are: human beings. Still, many men find that others—including potential partners—judge them by their appearance and force them into the old roles.

Men are just beginning to develop new roles that define masculinity in ways that are compatible with healthy life, healthy relationships, and recovery. For a while, some men are finding that the shift from old to new roles is causing confusion. In the end, though, it will bring greater freedom for both men and women.

Issues that many single, sober men face:

- Stereotypes of men
- Loss of child custody in divorce
- Financial pressures in divorce
- Guilt and shame over past victimization of sexual partners
- Fear of intimacy and commitment

Loss of Child Custody in Divorce. Men who have been divorced tend to face special challenges. Men more often than women are named the noncustodial parent. For the noncustodial parent, male or female, there is the sadness of seeing the children raised in another household. Drew speaks of the pain he feels every week when his children leave after their visit with him. He has doubts about his ex-wife's skills as a parent, but he's not sure what to do about it. And each time they leave, it feels as if a part of him is being torn away.

Financial Pressures in Divorce. In most divorces, both partners suffer financially, if only because it costs more to run two households than it does to run one. But men are still more likely to take a strong financial loss than women. Many men are financially drained through alimony and child support. Even those who are willing to shoulder this responsibility often have a hard time making ends meet.

For many men, the old stereotypical male roles don't work anymore. They just want to be who they are: human beings.

Guilt and Shame over Past Victimization of Sexual Partners. Most chemically dependent men have had some experience of sexually or physically abusing a sexual partner under the influence of mood-altering drugs. In sobriety, many men feel intense shame and guilt when they remember those experiences. Even in recovery, some men still use physical, sexual, and emotional aggression against their partners. Recovery from the role of the victimizer isn't an automatic side-benefit of sobriety. It often requires hard work in therapy and men's groups beyond the traditional sobriety-based recovery groups.

Fear of Intimacy and Commitment. Most men aren't as closely aware of their abandonment issues as women are. Our culture teaches many men to deal with their fears of abandonment through the "preemptive strike": Leave your partner before your partner has a chance to leave you. More men are aware of being afraid of intimacy and commitment. "Intimacy" might be defined as deep, close sharing of thoughts, feelings, and experiences. Intimacy isn't the same as sexual or sensual activity, although some people who are sexual together are also intimate together. Intimacy is frightening to people who have learned to fear their own softer emotions, like love and compassion. "Commitment" in relationships can be any number of things: a promise to be sexually faithful, a promise not to leave your partner, etc. But for some people, the possibility of commitment feels like the danger of being trapped in an uncomfortable situation with no way out.

Common Issues Facing Women	Common Issues Facing Men
The stereotype of the chemically dependent woman	Stereotypes of men
The stress of being the custodial parent	Loss of child custody in divorce
The superwoman syndrome	Financial pressures in divorce
Issues of sexual victimization	Guilt and shame over past victimization of sexual partners
Abandonment issues	Fear of intimacy and commitment

Many men have learned by example—from movies, television, books, friends, and adult role models—how to avoid intimacy. There are a thousand ways people can distract themselves and their partners from the growth of intimacy. Scott used to do it with anger and humor, whichever one seemed more appropriate at the time. He noticed that he was never able to feel really close to a woman, no matter how much he loved and desired her. In his singles recovery group, Scott slowly realized that his partners had been reaching out to him all the time, but that the closer they got, the more he dropped back into inappropriate humor or anger.

It's important to remember that many women also avoid intimacy, but they often use different tactics. Our culture teaches women that they're supposed to want and welcome intimacy. So many women who are afraid of intimacy learn to push it away by grasping it too hard. Donna couldn't understand why men kept drawing emotionally close to her, then pulling away after she started showing her feelings for them. In singles recovery, Donna learned that she had been acting very intimate too early in the relationships. One day she realized that she had been pushing her partners away by pushing too hard, as a way of coping with her own fear of getting close.

For men who have been widowed, fear of intimacy and commitment often clash with feelings of abandonment. Life becomes much more lonely than they expected. Researchers have found that women tend to become more independent and assertive after their husbands' death, but that widowed men tend to react in the opposite way. They often become less assertive and feel less complete. For men in general, grieving is difficult. Many of the emotions of grieving—sadness, depression, and guilt—are ones that men have been taught for centuries to pretend that they don't have. And crying is something that many men were "trained" not to do as they reached adolescence. There's more social encouragement for men to "drown their sorrows" with alcohol or escape into a fog with drugs. The problem is that the escape doesn't lock out the sorrow: instead, it locks the sorrow in, by keeping the grieving process from doing its healing work.

Thought and Discussion Questions

1. If you're a man, have you experienced problems connected with the old and new roles and stereotypes of men? How have these problems affected your life, your sobriety, and/or your relationships?
2. Are you a noncustodial parent? How have the problems associated with this role affected your life, your sobriety, and/or your relationships?
3. Have you suffered financially as a result of divorce? How have these problems affected your life,onships?

4. Do you have memories of victimizing sexual partners before sobriety, or in sobriety? How have feelings of guilt or shame over these experiences affected your life, your sobriety, and/or your relationships?
5. Have you ever experienced fear of intimacy or commitment? How have these fears affected your life, your sobriety, and/or your relationships?

Some Special Challenges for Gay Men and Lesbians

Gay men and lesbians face extra challenges in recovery. Along with society's long-held judgment of chemically dependent people and of people who are not married, they also have to contend with the prejudice and discrimination against gays and lesbians that still exists.

Extra Difficulty with Self-Acceptance

Acceptance of oneself, and the development of self-honesty, are more difficult when one's sexual identity has been the object of fear and ridicule since childhood. Often the alcohol and drug use began as a way to medicate the pain of self-hatred brought about by social pressure and prejudice.

> ### Some Special Challenges
> ### for Gay Men and Lesbians:
>
> - Extra difficulty with self-acceptance
> - Prejudice and lack of understanding by many straight people
> - Sense of not belonging in primarily straight recovery groups

Prejudice and Lack of Understanding

Because gay men were among the first groups of people in the United States to have high rates of HIV/AIDS infection, many straight (heterosexual) people's prejudice against both gay men and lesbians has deepened. In many cases it has even grown violent. In the face of all the prejudice, the gay community has often grown separate and isolated from straight society. Some relationship customs in gay society are different from those in straight society, but many are the same. There is little effective communication or understanding about similarities and differences. Straight people also tend to think that gay men and lesbians have the same issues to contend with, overlooking the differences that gender creates.

Sense of Not Belonging

It can be much harder for gays and lesbians to feel a sense of belonging in self-help groups whose members are mostly straight. Brian felt like a liar in his home group, even though he was telling the truth about his addiction. Whenever people would mention their wives or husbands, boyfriends or girlfriends, he felt isolated and different from everyone else. He knew he needed a sense of belonging in order to be healed, but he felt as if a glass wall separated him from the rest of the people at the meeting.

One night he mentioned his sexual identity in his comment, even though he feared that some or all members would shut him out. That didn't happen. A couple of the men seemed a little nervous around him after that, but most people acted exactly the same. One woman told him about a gay Alano club in her neighborhood. She said she often went to meetings there even though she was straight, because the meetings at the club were so good. When Brian became a regular at the club, he felt a sense of belonging that he'd never felt before. By making friends with both gay and straight people, he found a way to merge his recovering life with his life as a gay man.

All recovering people need strength, courage, dignity, and self-esteem to make it through the rough spots of recovery. For gay men and lesbians, getting sober in a society that still largely misunderstands and disapproves of them, these qualities are even more important.

The Presence of Hope

Now that we've looked at some of the challenges that singles face in recovery, it's important to remember that these problems all have solutions. The rest of this book will help you define your problems a little better and point you toward a number of possible solutions. As you undertake this journey of self-discovery, you'll learn more about the solutions that are right for you. Don't expect to understand or solve it all right away. It takes time. The book is organized in a way that lets you tackle these questions slowly and safely. You have a lot to gain by doing this work: relief from the pain of loneliness and failed relationships, the possibility of successful intimate relationships, and help for the most important relationship of all—your relationship with yourself.

Chapter
2

Preventing Relationship-Related Relapse

"There's something nobody's talking about, and I've got to talk about it," Felicia said at her home group. "And that's how many people in this community are relapsing over relationship stuff—even folks with some clean time. I just went to Mimi P's funeral, and she's never coming back. I don't want to go to any more funerals. I'm scared."

In this chapter, you'll look at common relationship-related relapse triggers:

- Getting into relationships in treatment
- Involvement with people who drink or drug
- Infatuation intoxication
- Isolation in the relationship
- The pain of disillusionment
- Fear of healthy intimacy
- Fear of being trapped or abandoned
- Conflict and/or abuse in the relationship
- Post-traumatic stress disorder
- The pain of breaking up

The relapse process is a complicated one that starts long before the person picks up a drink or a drug. There are many possible **relapse triggers**: situations or events a recovering person can use as an excuse to start or continue the relapse process. Relationships, and the issues that come up in relationships, are common relapse triggers.

Why are relationships such fertile ground for relapse? There are several reasons. First, they often tempt us to go into isolation with our partners, and isolation is an important part of chemical dependency and relapse. Relationships also raise many strong feelings. A chemically dependent person's longtime response to strong feelings is to medicate the unpleasant ones, and celebrate the positive ones, with alcohol or drugs. Relationships also raise our expectations, and drinking and drugging are the traditional ways of soothing disappointed expectations. And relationships make us vulnerable—open to the possibility of hurt and criticism. Chemical use is an excellent hiding place from our vulnerability as human beings.

Relationships are places of high vulnerability because they force us to confront the unfinished business from our childhood. This is a natural process and an important process for our overall growth and well-being. If you're not in a relationship, those old feelings and behaviors won't tend to come up for you very often. When you are in a relationship, though, you may find yourself feeling, saying, and doing things that are very uncomfortable. Often it's the old unresolved issues coming up. You'll need to work through these problems with your partner, your sponsor, and your therapist. Otherwise these issues can raise the risk of relapse, and damage your relationships.

Relapse Prevention

People who relapse often feel as if they had no choice. But really, the relapse process involves many decisions on the part of the person who relapses. Most of these decisions are *unconscious*: The person who's making them isn't aware of the decisions or of their possible effects. That makes them more dangerous. The **relapse prevention process** works to make people aware of the decisions they're making. That way, they have a chance of making different decisions, if they choose to do what it takes to avoid relapse.

> *In relapse prevention, people learn to manage their thoughts, feelings, urges, and actions in healthy ways. The first step is to become aware of your own relapse triggers and warning signs.*

The relapse process is often driven by irrational thoughts, unmanageable feelings, self-destructive urges, and self-defeating actions. In relapse prevention, people learn to manage their thoughts, feelings, urges, and actions in healthy ways. The first step is to become aware of your own common relapse triggers and warning signs. You can increase your awareness by coming up with relapse warning statements that are appropriate for you. A relapse warning statement starts with the words "I know I'm in trouble with my recovery when I...." For example, one warning statement might be "I know I'm in trouble with my recovery when I start skipping meetings to spend time with my partner."

If you've relapsed while in recovery from chemical dependence, you may need to begin a process of relapse prevention with a trained relapse prevention therapist (see the materials listed at the end of this book for more information and resources on relapse prevention). But in the meantime, this chapter will give you a brief overview of some of the relapse triggers often found in relationships.

Relationship-Related Relapse Triggers

The following are not the only relapse triggers brought on by relationships, but they're among the most common. As you read them, see if any of them match your experience.

Getting into Relationships in Treatment

The word "treatment" is used here to include the centers or hospitals where people go for chemical dependency treatment, self-help group meetings, therapy groups, and professional relationships with therapists or counselors. It's absolutely important that these settings feel—and be—completely safe for the recovering person. Any violation of safety is a betrayal of a sacred trust. It can trigger the relapse process. Unfortunately, many people's trust has been betrayed in these settings, at great danger to their recovery.

> **In treatment settings, there's great danger if you get involved with:**
> - Your sponsor or therapist
> - Someone in your regular self-help group or therapy group
> - Someone who's unstable in his or her recovery

Involvement with Your Therapist or Sponsor. Because of the closeness of the treatment relationship, many people develop romantic or sexual feelings for their counselors or therapists. This is normal and natural, but it can hurt the therapeutic process. Neil found it much harder to be honest with his therapist after he'd started having strong feelings for her. He didn't want to tell her about the feelings and life events that he was ashamed of. He wanted to impress her. When he felt like his recovery was being threatened, Neil finally told her how he was feeling, and asked her if he should be transferred to another therapist. They worked through the problem together.

Sometimes the therapist or counselor—or someone else who works for the treatment center or agency sponsoring therapeutic services—also flirts with a client or actually gets involved romantically or sexually. In all cases, this is inappropriate, a violation of professional ethics. Because the client is so vulnerable in therapy, he or she has less power than the therapist or other employee of the agency or center. Getting involved romantically or sexually with a client is a violation of power, even if the client really wants to get involved and the therapist has the best intentions. Sooner or later the client will realize that he or she has been betrayed and will be very vulnerable to relapse.

Trust and care is also important in the sponsorship relationship. Sexual and romantic involvement can destroy the safety of those relationships in short order. That's why straight people in recovery are urged to find sponsors of the same gender, and gay and bisexual people are urged to take care in choosing sponsors with whom there's no danger of involvement.

Involvement with Members of Therapy or Self-Help Groups. At self-help and therapy group meetings, it's also important to keep sex and romance out of the picture, especially when people are new to recovery. And in a therapy group, it's important not to flirt or get involved no matter how long both people have been in recovery. For the reasons described in the next few pages, even healthy relationships can trigger relapse in people whose recovery is shaky in any way. That's where the AA folk wisdom came from that says "no relationships in the first year."

> *Knowing that someone is newly recovering gives*
> *people a responsibility to keep their attraction*
> *and their desire to themselves. Unfortunately,*
> *some people deny that responsibility.*

That's also why the "thirteenth step" is so dangerous. Officially, there are only twelve steps in programs like Alcoholics Anonymous, etc. But the term "thirteenth step" has been given to the act of getting involved with someone who is newly recovering. When someone has a sexual or romantic encounter or relationship with someone who is new to the program (or newly back from a relapse), it's a betrayal of the unspoken promise in recovery groups: "We're here to support and promote one another's recovery. We're not here to use one another."

Knowing that someone is newly recovering gives people a responsibility to keep their attraction and their desire to themselves. Unfortunately, at meetings there are people who deny that responsibility and actually seek out newcomers as possible romantic partners. These people are often thought of as predators.

At one AA meeting, the problem was getting so bad that the young women started working together to protect new women as they entered the group. Before and after meetings, they would stand in a circle around the newcomers, as if to shield them from attack. During the meetings, they would sit on either side of them. They would even go up to the predatory men in the group and say "Leave this one alone." It worked.

> *If someone is shaky in his or her recovery, the worst thing you can do—for yourself and for the other person—is to get involved sexually or romantically.*

Involvement with People Whose Recovery Is Shaky. Many people in therapy and self-help groups have a hard time making and keeping a commitment to sobriety. They might have chronic relapse problems that have never been addressed properly. They might have severe psychological effects from their experiences in childhood or during their drinking or drugging years, or chemical imbalances that haven't been diagnosed or treated. Many people need more help than they're willing or able to accept right now. That doesn't keep them from being bright, energetic, and attractive. In fact, it sometimes adds to the attraction: Their needs are so great that there's a strong temptation to try to supply the love and attention that they want so desperately.

If someone is shaky in his or her recovery, the worst thing you can do—for yourself and for the other person—is to get involved sexually or romantically. Many people have relapsed because their partners relapsed and they were dragged down in the current. No relationship is worth a relapse, no matter how wonderful the person is. And no recovering addict or alcoholic is immune from relapse. When someone you're involved with is drinking or drugging, even on the sly, it's very hard to keep your own recovery safe. Your partner might use alcohol or drugs in your presence, or might smell of those substances after using and trigger your cravings. And you can bet that your partner will be thinking and acting in "crazy," self-defeating ways in the relationship.

If you're telling yourself that you can help someone's recovery by getting involved with him or her, *you're wrong*. Under the best circumstances, romantic and sexual relationships are difficult. They add stress to our lives, rather than taking it away. If someone is shaky, getting into a relationship will shake him or her up even more.

Thought and Discussion Questions

1. What are some ways you feel vulnerable to romantic relationships in the early weeks and months of recovery?

2. Have you ever been sexually or romantically involved with, or been invited to get involved with, your therapist, sponsor, or an employee of a treatment center where you're getting services? What happened as a result?

3. What way of responding to this kind of invitation would best protect the safety of the recovering person?

4. Have you ever experienced, seen, or heard of newly recovering people being "hit on" by others in their group sessions or meetings? Please describe these incidents.

5. What are some effective ways of handling these kinds of situations?

6. Have you ever tried to start sexual or romantic contact with someone in your therapy group, or someone in his or her first year of recovery? Please describe this.

7. In what ways could this situation be dangerous, for you and for the other person?

8. A relapse warning statement starts with the words "I know I'm in trouble with my recovery when I...." For example, one warning statement might be, "I know I'm in trouble with my recovery when I start checking out all the attractive people at my meetings and having fantasies about them." Finish this relapse warning statement regarding relationships in therapy or early recovery: "I know I'm in trouble with my recovery when I...."

Involvement with People Who Drink or Drug

As dangerous as it is to get involved with people whose recovery is shaky, it's even more dangerous to get—or stay—involved with someone who's not in recovery and uses alcohol or drugs addictively. These relationships are usually full of turmoil and conflict, often abusive. The alcohol and drugs may be out in plain sight, triggering cravings for the partner who's trying to recover. The nonrecovering partner often feels jealous of and threatened by the recovery program, recovering friends, and sponsors and therapists.

Like alcohol and other drugs, infatuation distracts us from the pain of everyday living. It gives us something to think about, even when it would be more productive to think about other things.

Even relationships with nonaddicted people who drink or use occasionally can be dangerous, if they continue to drink or use in your presence. Some recovering people who still have shame issues over being addicted are reluctant to tell potential partners about their addiction. Instead, they make excuses for not drinking alcohol or using other drugs. This practice is very dangerous. It keeps them exposed to the substances that might trigger cravings and relapse. It also destroys the honesty that is so necessary for a healthy relationship.

Infatuation Intoxication

Believe it or not, infatuation is a mood-altering drug. During the first couple months of a relationship, the brain releases chemicals that work on our moods very much like drugs. Like alcohol and other drugs, infatuation distracts us from the pain of everyday living. It gives us something to think about, even when it would be more productive to think about other things. This can trigger the urge to go back to the other drugs that used to produce those same feelings.

When Nikki fell for Patrick, she was a little scared by the intensity of her positive feelings. She loved those feelings, but she wasn't used to feeling so good without drinking or using. Sometimes she'd feel hopeless, too, wondering if he could possibly love her back. The fear of losing him—or never really having him—was so strong that she began to have cravings for cocaine, just to get her confidence up.

Thought and Discussion Questions

1. What does infatuation feel like to you?
2. How is that similar to the way alcohol or other drugs felt?
3. In what ways might the feelings of infatuation trigger urges to drink or use?
4. Finish the following relapse warning statement about infatuation: "I know I'm in trouble with my recovery when I...."

Isolation in the Relationship

Chemically dependent people tend to have a problem with isolation. Isolation can happen when you're all alone, or it can happen in a room full of people. It's a way of cutting yourself off from help, support, and accurate information about your behavior. Isolation feeds the disease of addiction, just as exposure to healthy recovering people feeds recovery.

> *Having a relationship with a sober person is not a legitimate substitute for meetings, therapy sessions, or talks with your sponsor.*

In the early days of a relationship, it's common to want to spend more and more time alone with your partner. If you're in recovery for chemical dependency, you can even try to use your partner to take the place of the drink or the drug. Henry and Margo fell in love so quickly and deeply that nobody ever thought they'd come up for air. They shut themselves inside for whole weekends at a time, and stopped showing up at their meetings.

Having a relationship with a sober person is not a legitimate substitute for meetings, therapy sessions, or talks with your sponsor. It's not the same. You need exposure to many different people and the magic that happens when people are together *only* for the purpose of staying sober. In a relationship, you have many purposes. The isolation that many people create around their relationships has triggered many a relapse.

Thought and Discussion Questions

1. How have you tried to protect yourself by isolating?
2. How have you tried to protect your relationships by isolating with your partner?
3. What role did isolation play in your drinking or drug use?
4. How do you isolate in your current relationship, or how have you isolated in past relationships?
5. What are some ways of breaking out of your isolation in relationships?
6. Why is isolation dangerous for you in relationships?
7. Complete the following relapse warning statement regarding isolation in relationships: "I know I'm in trouble in my recovery when I...."

The Pain of Disillusionment

Before a relationship starts, and even in its early stages, it's easy to have high expectations of what the relationship will mean in our lives. Rocky believed that a good relationship would make a lot of his problems go away. It would give him higher self-esteem and a sense of meaning and purpose. He would start keeping his apartment clean. Hey, maybe she'd even clean his apartment for him! His career would improve, because he'd be more confident and complete.

After he'd been involved with Theresa for a while, Rocky started asking himself what was going on. He still felt like a jerk a lot of the time. His place was still messy. He was still on probation at work. He and Theresa were reasonably happy, but it hadn't affected any of those areas of his life at all. True, if he needed to complain about something, she would listen and understand. But she didn't fix anything for him by being in his life.

> *Before you even approach a relationship, you'll need to look honestly and realistically at your expectations.*

The Fantasy Bond. A major trigger for disillusionment is what is called the "fantasy bond." In this process you create an unrealistic perception of who your partner is and project it onto your partner. You see your partner as the person you want him or her to be, rather than who your partner really is. Then you become disillusioned when you see the real person, with all their flaws and shortcomings. This is a common process for alcoholics and addicts, even in recovery.

Expecting Love to Conquer All. Another disillusionment trigger is based on the expectation that love will "cure everything." "If I fall in love, all my problems will work out." Many people have been trained in this expectation by unrealistic movie and television plots, where all the heroes' troubles are resolved and the happy couple lives happily ever after. As the song says, "Love hurts." It's important to stick to relationships that are nonabusive, but even healthy relationships often bring out more problems than they solve. If you enter a relationship expecting it to fix you or your problems, you're setting yourself up for disappointment and the danger of relapse. According to an anonymous quote in a recovery magazine, "Expectations are premeditated resentments."

Depending on how high your expectations are, the reality of a relationship can be quite a letdown. This is especially true when both partners start pushing one another's buttons in some of the ways that will be described later in this book. If your response to disappointment and disillusionment is to think about drinking or drugging, you're in trouble. Before you even approach a relationship, you'll need to look honestly and realistically at your expectations.

Thought and Discussion Questions

1. What are (or have been) some of your expectations or fantasies about what a relationship will do for you, your life, or your sobriety?
2. In what ways have your expectations or fantasies been fulfilled in past relationships?
3. What's your most common reaction when your expectations are disappointed?
4. What's a more constructive reaction that you might try?
5. Complete the following relapse warning statement regarding expectations in relationships: "I know I'm in trouble with my recovery when I...."

Fear of Healthy Intimacy

The fear of healthy intimacy is an issue that you probably didn't have to face when you were out there in active addiction. You could hide behind the mask of alcohol or drugs. You didn't have to state the simple, honest truth about who you were, what you were thinking, and how you felt. Under the influence, you could either hide your thoughts and feelings inside, or blurt them out in a rage or a fit of emotion.

If you haven't addressed your fear of intimacy through hard work in recovery and therapy, romantic relationships can be terrifying. Sally started to get into a relationship in her second year of recovery, but found herself using every emotional trick to push her partner away. "Wow," she said to herself when her tears had quieted down for a while. "Maybe I'm not ready to get that close to anyone yet." If she had forced herself to get into that relationship, it would have put her in some dangerous patterns of thinking, feeling, and acting. She would have been raising her risk of relapse.

Thought and Discussion Questions

1. What's your first reaction to people who are friendly to you?
2. How do you tend to respond to people who get too close, too soon? (What do you say, and what do you do?)
3. How do you express interest in another person? (What do you say, and what do you do?)
4. How do you feel when someone you're interested in doesn't return your interest? (What do you say, and what do you do?)
5. Complete the following relapse warning statement regarding the fear of intimacy in relationships: "I know I'm in trouble with my recovery when I...."

Fear of Being Trapped or Abandoned

Many recovering people have strong fears of being trapped in relationships or abandoned by their partners, based on experiences they had in childhood and in active addiction. Some people have an all-or-nothing response to relationships: "If I'm going to get involved, it has to develop very quickly and grow very intense." This is based on their lack of skill in recognizing, communicating, and protecting their own needs, wants, and limits. They don't have a clear sense of the psychological boundaries between their lives and their partners', and they lack assertiveness and self-protection skills. Because they can't trust themselves to set and defend their boundaries, they can't trust their partners not to trap them in the wrong relationships.

The abandonment issues mentioned in the previous chapter also serve as strong relationship-related relapse triggers. Not only do those fears compel people to stay in inappropriate relationships, but they can also create intense emotional pressure for both partners in appropriate relationships. With any extreme upset, there is the possibility that people will turn to their traditional ways of coping with emotional discomfort. For recovering addicts and alcoholics, this might trigger thoughts of drinking or using.

Conflict and/or Abuse in the Relationship

Few recovering people are comfortable with conflict, and fewer still have effective conflict management skills. This is true even of the people who appear to get into conflict most easily or most often. Brad thought he was comfortable with conflict because he got into arguments so often and could fly into a rage at a moment's notice. Then his sponsor reminded him that those tendencies were really evidence that he was very uncomfortable with conflict. He used his temper as a way of shielding himself from the difficult fact that other people disagreed with him and didn't always do what he wanted them to do.

Many people start the relapse process because they don't know how to cope effectively with conflict in their relationships. They take a drink or a drug as a way of punishing their partners for doing or saying things that hurt them.

Physical, Sexual, and Emotional Abuse. Many people in violent or abusive relationships turn to relapse as their only hope of medicating the pain of those relationships. In these cases, relapse is tragic and unnecessary. After the drink or the drug has worn off, the relationships are still painful, and the effects of relapse add to that pain. Alcohol and other drugs are often used to justify abusing others or tolerating their abuse. This is true for physical, sexual, and emotional violence and abuse.

For men who have histories of abusing their partners, the guilt, shame, and embarrassment over those experiences can be a strong relapse trigger. Their anger against women might have been born long before they began using alcohol and other drugs. In most cases the abusive behavior doesn't stop just because they stop using those substances. Specific treatment for the abusive and/or violent behavior is necessary, as soon as possible.

Many people in violent or abusive relationships turn to relapse as their only hope of medicating the pain of those relationships. In these cases, relapse is tragic and unnecessary.

Issues of abuse and violence between the genders are closely tied in with issues of self-worth and violations of dignity and respect. A complicated set of factors leads people to abuse others, or to stay in relationships where they are being abused. If you have a history of abusing others or being abused, you'll need to address those issues in recovery and in therapy. If the issues aren't addressed directly and effectively, they raise your risk of relapse significantly.

There are many better ways of coping with conflict, violence, and abuse in relationships than relapse. There are self-help groups, therapy groups, sponsors, and therapists. There are also many ways of avoiding relationships until you know how to cope with abuse and conflict effectively.

Thought and Discussion Questions

1. How did you respond to conflict when you were actively addicted?

2. How do you usually respond to conflict now that you're in recovery?

3. Do you actively seek conflict? Please explain.

4. Do you try to avoid conflict? Please explain.

5. What might be a more effective way of dealing with conflict?

6. Complete the following relapse warning statement regarding conflict in your relationships: "I know I'm in trouble with my recovery when I...."

7. Have you ever been abused by partners, or abused partners in your relationships? How might the memory of that abuse affect your current or future relationships?

8. If you're currently in an abusive relationship—as the abuser or the one being abused—what are some steps you might take to get help? Who could you contact to find out what steps to take?

Post-Traumatic Stress Disorder

Later in this book you'll be reading about post-traumatic stress disorder (PTSD). It's being mentioned briefly here because it's such a common and powerful relapse trigger. PTSD is a set of symptoms caused by past experiences of intense fear, abuse, pain, or violence. Common sources of PTSD include physical, sexual, or emotional abuse in childhood; exposure to violence in the community; physical or sexual victimization in adulthood; and the effects of combat.

PTSD symptoms include:

- nightmares
- flashbacks
- loss of sleep
- hypervigilance
- depression

- numbness
- anger
- anxiety
- fear

Symptoms of PTSD include nightmares or intense waking memories called "flashbacks," loss of sleep, being jumpy or easily startled (called "hypervigilance"), depression, numbness, anger, anxiety, and fear. Sometimes alcohol and drugs have been used to "medicate" those symptoms. In recovery, many people find the memories and other symptoms returning, and they don't know how to cope. Although relapse is a common response to PTSD symptoms, there are other options. If you begin to experience any of these symptoms—or if you think you might be experiencing them—it's important to get professional help from a therapist who knows how to work with PTSD.

The Pain of Breaking Up

Carrie knew she shouldn't call Bob. They'd broken up a week before and she knew he'd made up his mind, but she just had to try. When she called him and all but begged him to try again, she felt humiliated. In a cool and distant voice, he told her that he couldn't. It was over. She headed for the nearest bar. Later, in talking it through with her relapse prevention therapist, Carrie realized that she had called him—not only to make one last desperate try—but also to push herself closer to relapse.

> *Recovering people who get through breakups*
> *without relapsing actually end up feeling less pain*
> *than the people who drink or use, because they*
> *don't have to deal with all the pain of relapse.*

Experience in active addiction says that you can't get through a time of major pain and disappointment without taking a drink or a drug. Television and movies even tell you that, with all the examples they show. The pain of breaking up is a powerful relapse trigger. Of course, many recovering people get through breakups without relapsing. They actually end up feeling less pain than the people who drink or use because they don't have to deal with all the pain of relapse.

"When Roger left, I thought about taking a drink for the first time in years," said Marianne in her comment at an AA meeting. "Then I did what they tell us to do. I played out the whole scene in my head. First I'd have a drink, then I'd finish the bottle. Then I'd have to get another bottle, because one was never enough for me. Then eventually there would be the hangover, and all the puking, and all the humiliation. Then if I was lucky, I'd come back in here and tell you I'd slipped. And you'd welcome me back and love me and everything, but I'd still feel really ashamed...," she paused for a moment, "...and he'd still be gone."

Thought and Discussion Questions

1. Describe the way you used to react to a breakup when you were actively addicted.

2. If you've been through a breakup in recovery, describe the way you reacted to it. (If you haven't, describe the way you think you might react if it happened tomorrow.)

3. What might be a more effective way of reacting to a breakup?

4. If you were to relapse, what do you think your life would be like?

5. Complete the following relapse warning statement regarding a possible breakup-related relapse: "I know I'm in trouble with my recovery when I...."

Chapter
3

An Inventory of Past Relationships

"What happened?" Joy asked her singles recovery group. "I feel like I've come out of a fog, and I see all this wreckage behind me. What did I do to my relationships? What did they do to me?"

In this chapter, you'll look at:

- Honesty and responsibility in relationships
- The major issues that come up in relationships with active addicts
- Relationships through the stages of addiction

Many recovering people ask themselves these kinds of questions. At first the past might seem like a jumble of unconnected experiences, impossible to understand. But time, healing, and honest attention to the past will reveal a number of patterns. Those patterns will make the past more understandable, and understanding the past is the first step toward building a much better future.

Honesty and Responsibility in Relationship Recovery

This chapter is meant to start you off on an honest inventory of your past relationships. This inventory doesn't replace the fourth step of AA, NA, CA, etc., in which you look honestly at your past life in general, and at your strengths, weaknesses, and motivations. However, the relationship inventory can help you with your fourth step, or pick up where your fourth-step inventory left off.

When you were actively drinking and using, there were probably many times when putting honesty aside seemed necessary for survival. Now in recovery, you learn that the honesty itself is what's necessary for your survival. For example, if you can't be honest about having a problem and needing help, you might neglect your program and have a relapse. And honesty is just as necessary for the health and survival of your relationships.

Honesty with other people gets a little complicated: There are some pieces of honest information you'll want to hold back—like the fact that you hate your boss's new haircut—because that information isn't necessary, useful, or kind. But honesty with yourself is different. It has to be absolute, to the best of your ability at the time. The truth tends to reveal itself in layers. You can't see yourself as clearly and honestly after one month's sobriety as you can at your one-year anniversary, and at five years you can see much more. The important thing is to be willing, at each stage of recovery, to look honestly at each new insight as it is revealed to you.

Thought and Discussion Questions

1. What's an example of a time before recovery when you really felt that your physical or emotional survival depended on "bending" or sacrificing the truth?

2. What's an example in your life today of something you have to be honest about in order to be healthy and survive?

3. What's one example in your life today of something you must be honest about in order to be healthy in recovery?

4. Before you entered recovery, how did your dishonesty hurt or destroy an important relationship? (Give one example.)

Replacing Guilt and Shame with Responsibility

The next thing to do is to avoid falling into the guilt-and-shame trap. When we realize what we've done wrong and start beating ourselves up about it, we might think that's the way to take responsibility for our mistakes. But it's not. Think of the last time someone admitted doing something that hurt or inconvenienced you. Chances are their guilt was useless to you. What you really wanted was for them to take responsibility for their actions and, if possible, make it up to you.

Responsibility is different from guilt and shame in some important ways. Guilt is often described as the feeling that you've made a mistake, and shame as the feeling that you *are* a mistake. But guilt also implies that you're carrying the mark of a wrong done in the past. If you take responsibility, though, it's for your mistakes and for your successes, in the past, present, and future. Few people really want to be described as a guilty person or a shameful person. But most of us want to be described as a responsible person.

> *Few people really want to be described as a guilty person or a shameful person. But most of us want to be described as a responsible person.*

The ninth step, in which we repair the damage we have caused in our lives, says that we "made direct amends to such people...." It doesn't say we "apologized to such people" or "groveled before such people." We took responsibility for what we had done and did our best to repair the damage. And the tenth step (a daily and spot-check inventory of ourselves) says "when we were wrong, promptly admitted it," not "when we were wrong, felt really terrible about it." So as you read through this chapter and think about what your addiction has done to your relationships, do it in the spirit of responsibility. Taking responsibility can free you from the pain of guilt.

One more request: As you read this chapter and answer the questions, if it raises painful or frightening emotions, put it down for a while. Talk to your sponsor or your therapist about your reactions. If it's more comfortable to do so, read through this chapter with a friend you can trust (but not with a romantic partner). If the chapter brings up memories of painful events that you'd forgotten or never knew you'd been through, skip this chapter for now, and make sure you have a therapist who can help you cope with those memories. If you keep working on your recovery, you'll have plenty of time to heal your old relationship patterns. Right now, though, your safety is more important.

Thought and Discussion Questions

1. What's your definition of "guilt"?
2. What do you do (how do you act) when you feel guilty?
3. What's your definition of "shame"?
4. What do you do (how do you act) when you feel ashamed?
5. How do guilt and shame affect your relationships?
6. Give two examples of irresponsible things you have done.
7. Give two examples of responsible things you have done.

Issues that Arise in Relationships with Active Addicts

If you've been in recovery for even a little while, you know that your addictive behaviors included much more than just picking up too many drinks, joints, pipes, or needles. When you were "out there," you probably knew you had problems in your life, but you had no idea how many of those problems were related to the drinking and drugging. Many of those problems affected your romantic and sexual relationships. When relationships failed, it was easier to blame your partner or to make a blanket statement like "I'm no good at relationships." What you probably weren't ready to admit was that your relationship with alcohol or drugs was so important to you that you were willing to let your other relationships suffer.

> **Common characteristics of relationships in addiction:**
>
> • Dependence
> • Codependence
> • Control
> • Distrust

No doubt your partners also did many things that added to the problems. Partners who are close to chemically dependent people often take on a number of unhealthy thoughts and behaviors to cope with the disease. But no matter what your partners said or did, your own actions helped destroy relationships you were hoping would last, kept you in destructive relationships that you knew weren't good for you, or forced you into isolation with your addictive disease. Here are some of the areas of relationships that chemical dependency often affects.

Dependence

Understandably, addiction does strange things to both partners' need and ability to depend on one another. Chemically dependent people come to depend too much on the drug, and at the same time they deny or ignore the responsibilities that get in the way of drinking or using. This can lead them to lean too much on their romantic partners, who sometimes step in to take care of those responsibilities. It can also lead chemically dependent people to push romantic partners away, because those partners' needs get in the way of the relationship with the substance. Remember the counterdependent (tough) personality style discussed in the first chapter? Many addicted people who have that type of personality tend to push their partners away emotionally, to hide the fact that their addiction is creating intense needs in other areas of their lives. They become the center of the universe, ignoring their partners' needs.

> **No matter what your partner said or did, your own actions helped:**
> - destroy relationships you were hoping would last
> - keep you in destructive relationships
> - force you into isolation

Codependence

Many partners of chemically dependent people also take on strange reactions to their partners' dependence. People who have a codependent (soft) personality style tend to be attracted to counterdependent addicted people. They step in to take care of the responsibilities that their addicted partners have cast aside, often ignoring their own needs and responsibilities. In many cases people with codependent personality styles were raised in troubled families where their emotional survival depended on meeting other people's needs. But even some people who weren't raised with these codependent coping skills can develop a codependent style if they spend much time in relationship with counterdependent chemically dependent people.

> **Chemically dependent people tend to:**
> - depend too much on the drug
> - ignore or push away their responsibilities
> - push their partners away
> - become the center of their own universe
>
> **Codependent people tend to:**
> - accept that they can't depend on their partner
> - take over their partner's responsibilities
> - cling to their partner
> - make their partner the center of the universe

Brittany and Peter appeared to have the perfect relationship. She was outgoing and magnetic; he was quiet and calm, and he enjoyed watching her shine. Their friends and families marveled at how funny and captivating she was, and how devoted he was. Only one friend, an alcoholism counselor, noticed that Peter's attention to Brittany often had the quality of a skilled servant, anticipating her needs before she had a chance to state them. And sometimes he seemed a little like the attentive parent of a toddler, moving things out of her way so she wouldn't knock them over, coaxing her toward the door when she'd had too much to drink, and always taking the wheel when it was time to go home. Because she was often protected from the consequences of her drinking, Brittany was able to pretend she didn't have a problem.

People who take on codependent roles often appear to be doing all they can to preserve the closeness of their relationships. In his eagerness to take care of Brittany, Peter seemed almost needy—dependent on her dependence on him. In reality, though, the intensity of his need tended to make her want more distance from him, because she knew how unbalanced the relationship was. His codependence was pushing her away as surely as her reliance on the alcohol pushed him away.

Thought and Discussion Questions

1. What are two ways you've used alcohol or drugs to "push" people away?
2. What are two ways you or your partner have sacrificed your personal needs, or neglected your responsibilities, in order to "take care of" the other?
3. If you were the one sacrificing your needs and responsibilities, how did you feel? If your partner was the one, how did he or she feel?
4. When you were drinking and using, what were at least two ways others protected you from the consequences of your addiction?

Control

Along with issues of dependence come issues of control. For the codependent partner who's taking on some of his or her partner's responsibilities, the reward or "payoff" is a funny kind of control. Of course, it doesn't feel like control, because the addicted partner is so often unpredictable and out of control. But the codependent partner has control of many of the practical areas of the chemically dependent partner's life—like whether or not this partner is guided into bed before he or she passes out. If they've been hurt or inconvenienced by their addicted partners' actions, codependent partners can also use guilt as a way of getting their partners to do what they want.

Codependent partners tend to:
- control many practical areas of the addicted partner's life
- use guilt as a way of manipulating their partners

Counterdependent people tend to control their partners:
- physically, through force or threats of force
- emotionally, through criticism or ridicule
- intellectually, by trying to make them feel stupid

Counterdependent people who are addicted also tend to have a strong need to feel in control, because their addiction has caused them to lose control of some of their own responsibilities. In some cases they might try to control their partners *physically* (by using physical or sexual force, or by threatening to hurt them), *emotionally* (by putting them down or making fun of them), or *intellectually* (by doing or saying things to make them feel wrong or stupid).

When Clair started dating Frank, she fell quickly for his strength and his intelligence. He helped her out of an abusive relationship with a drug dealer, and she moved in with him. She soon started to realize that he drank and drugged a lot and sometimes let his job, housework, and finances go. She stepped in quietly to help in a lot of areas, and he was grateful. She also noticed that his opinions were very important to him, and he would sometimes get mad at her if she disagreed with him—especially in front of other people. She started feeling afraid of what he thought of her, and tried to say what he would want her to say. The more she did that, the less he seemed to respect her. After he would say or do things that hurt her, he would often admit he was wrong and grow very sorry and loving. She knew that deep down he really needed and relied on her, and that gave her some satisfaction.

Thought and Discussion Questions

1. Before you entered recovery, what were two ways you tried to "control" your partner's actions?
2. How did your partner react when you used these control techniques?
3. How did your actions, and your partners' reactions, affect the closeness in your relationship?

Distrust

One of the most common ways of trying to control people is by lying, shading the truth, or holding back information that they have a right to know. For that reason, the way people in chemically dependent relationships handle control issues often leads to problems in the area of trust. Often two people start out having a hard time trusting one another because of experiences in childhood and with past partners. The denial, dishonesty, and control issues that come with addiction make it even harder for appropriate trust to develop and grow. Inability to trust—and the forces that make it hard to trust—tend to destroy relationships.

Jackie and Dan were both weekend drinkers and users when they met, and they enjoyed sharing that part of their lives. As the months passed, Jackie fell into heavier and more frequent use. Ashamed, she tried to hide her use from Dan and would make excuses for not seeing him during the week. Dan felt neglected, but he was too proud to tell Jackie and too much involved to break off the relationship. Out of anger, he started seeing other women "on the sly," even though he and Jackie had made a commitment to be sexually faithful to one another. Each one was hiding important information because they didn't trust one another enough to be honest. And in hiding this information, each one destroyed what was left of the other one's trust.

> *The denial, dishonesty, and control issues that come with addiction make it even harder for appropriate trust to develop and grow. This tends to destroy relationships.*

Some people also have the opposite problem: trusting the wrong people too much. In the alcohol and drug cultures, there are plenty of people who don't care who they hurt, use, or betray. Many chemically dependent people have been drawn into relationships with people who hurt them physically, sexually, emotionally, or financially. They've entered into these relationships with the same denial that makes it possible to keep using alcohol and drugs despite all the signs that their use is causing serious problems in their lives. Some people enter into the same destructive relationship over and over again, with the same partner or with different partners each time. Often this pattern destroys their ability to trust—and sometimes they'll swear off relationships entirely—but when they do fall for someone, it's usually the same partner in sheep's clothing.

A person who's operating in a healthy way will start a relationship by holding back a lot of personal information and emotional investment. An emotionally healthy partner will be suspicious of someone who tells too much too quickly. It's important to test the relationship a little at a time to see if it's safe to share a little more information or care a little bit more. If your partner proves himself or herself worthy of trust, then you get involved a little more deeply, and you don't hold back important secrets that your partner has a right to know. If your partner betrays your trust, then you pull back or get out of the relationship.

> *Some people enter into the same destructive relationship over and over again, with the same partner or with different partners each time.*

Alcohol and some other drugs make it harder to hold back information and emotions. Under the influence, Bridget felt as if she could trust Norm completely and believed they were sharing true intimacy. Once they had told each other some very personal things, she felt they were so close that she had no right to deny him sex. When she woke up the next day, she realized she had told him a lot of embarrassing details about herself, and she had rushed into sex before she felt good about it. Feeling ashamed and guilty, she now regretted having shared so much with him.

In general, people with chemical dependency tend to be attracted to other chemically dependent people and to codependent people. This lowers their chance of building healthy relationship skills because it keeps them in the company of people whose ways of relating are as unhealthy as theirs.

Thought and Discussion Questions

1. Before you entered recovery, what were two ways you showed that you didn't trust your partner?
2. Describe at least three qualities that attracted you to past partners.
3. Did these qualities end up causing problems in your relationships? If so, describe how that happened.

Relationships and Addiction

Addiction is a progressive disease. As your addiction progressed, so did the damage to your relationships. Chemical dependency is often mapped out in three stages: early-, middle-, and late- or chronic-stage addiction. The rest of this section looks at the most common types of relationship damage in each of those stages.

Relationships in the Early Stage of Addiction

In the early stage, addiction doesn't appear to have a lot of negative consequences. People are still drinking and using drugs to feel good and get high, so they feel like their use is under control. Their social lives revolve around the places where they use: bars, clubs, parties, friends' houses, home, etc. They often seek out partners who fit into those situations and are willing to drink and use with them. Then they can fool one another into believing their use is normal.

> **Common relationship issues in the early stage of addiction:**
> * Confusion of love with the feeling of being high
> * Discomfort when only one partner is using
> * Communication issues
> * Honesty issues
> * Honesty and self-honesty about sexual intentions and limits

Confusion of Love with the Feeling of Being High. Many addicted people have little or no recent experience in sexual or romantic relationships without the influence of alcohol or drugs. When they're with their partners, especially in social or sexual situations, they're high. Over time, they learn to confuse feelings of love with the feeling of being high. Many feelings that pass for love are really the effects of the chemicals. The high becomes an important part of the relationship. An important effect of this is that, when they fall in love in sobriety, they expect it to feel the same as it did in active addiction. Because they're not high, it doesn't feel the same, and so they decide that it can't be love.

Discomfort When One Partner Doesn't Use. If one partner doesn't use—or uses much less—the other partner has two options, neither of them very comfortable. One option is to drink or use with the partner anyway, knowing that they'll be operating on different levels of consciousness. This can create distance in the relationship. The other option is to try to control the drinking and drugging around the partner, pretending to be a more moderate user. This kind of dishonesty opens the door to other kinds of dishonesty in the relationship. It's also easy to resent the partner who doesn't drink or use addictively, as if that partner is to blame for the trouble and discomfort of hiding or cutting down the use of alcohol or drugs.

Communication Issues. There are many kinds of communication that don't happen, or don't happen effectively, when people are drinking and using addictively. In relationships, the most important kind of communication is honest information about your true thoughts, feelings, and actions.

Communication in relationships is hard under any circumstance. After the infatuation wears off, the little differences between people that once looked charming start to look annoying. These issues can blow up into huge misunderstandings if they aren't dealt with calmly, carefully, and honestly. Calm, care, and honesty are much harder to find when one is under the influence. Instead, hurt feelings and little resentments are often stuffed inside until they explode over something completely unrelated. Alcohol and other drugs make it harder not to speak or act in anger, even if those actions include violence.

Ben was still in the early stage of addiction when his fights with his wife, Georgine, started escalating into violence. The fights would always start over something silly, but they had all the force of the hurt and tension that had been building for months. He didn't hit her every time he drank; but every time he hit her, he'd been drinking. The first few times, Georgine told herself he'd never hit her again, but after her sister noticed a bruise on her arm, she had to admit that there was a problem. After their next violent fight, she found the courage to tell him she'd leave him if he didn't go into treatment for his alcoholism. In treatment, Ben's counselor told him he'd also need separate treatment and ongoing support for his violent impulses. When he finished treatment, Ben joined AA and started going to a weekly batterers therapy group. He and Georgine also started couples counseling to learn how to cope with their differences.

> *Calm, care, and honesty are much harder to find under the influence. Hurt feelings and little resentments are often stuffed inside until they explode over something completely unrelated.*

Honesty Issues. Another all-important art of communication is each partner's willingness and ability to be honest and open about what he or she does or doesn't want from the relationship. This kind of honesty is easier to avoid when one or both partners are drunk, high, or suffering from hangovers most of the time. Linda and Dean were both romantic by nature, so they had a lot of romance in their relationship—roses and champagne, lobster and champagne, soft music and champagne, bubble baths and cocaine—but they never talked about what the romance meant. Linda wanted a long-term, committed relationship in her life, but she didn't want to say it straight out for fear of scaring Dean away. Dean just wanted a short-term romantic fantasy, but he didn't want to say so for fear of losing Linda's company. Linda tried to bring up the subject a couple of times, but Dean managed to escape her questions in the alcoholic fog and the euphoria from the cocaine. After a while Linda started picking fights with Dean, and the relationship broke up. Neither partner really understood or said why the relationship had failed.

*Alcohol lowers our ability to predict conse-
quences, control our aggression, and communicate clearly about our limits.*

**Honesty and Self-Honesty about Sexual Intentions and
Limits**. One dangerous problem is the difficulty many people have
talking honestly about their sexual limits—the point beyond which
they're not willing to go with this partner at this time. This is difficult even without the influence of alcohol and drugs. When one
or more partners is sexually attracted, it's hard to resist our sexual
urges long enough to think about the possible effects of our actions. It's equally hard to see the danger signs in partners who
might be sexually aggressive or violent, and to say no to partners
who are using lies and other kinds of manipulation to try to get
us to say yes. And many people find it difficult to refuse to have
sex without protection against HIV/AIDS and other sexually trans-
mitted diseases.

When people are in the habit of drinking and using
addictively, these kinds of protective skills become even harder
to learn and use. Alcohol lowers our ability to predict consequences, control our aggression, and communicate clearly about
our limits. Even in the early stage of addiction, denial is already
a powerful force. Many people are raped, manipulated, or robbed
by people they thought were safe partners. And many contract
the HIV virus from people who seemed at very low risk of having the virus. Often people come out of blackouts (periods of
lost memory) to find out that they had sex—or wonder if they
had sex—with the wrong person. Many people have been raped
while in blackouts—or even after they had passed out—by partners who used their drunk or unconscious state as an excuse to
rape them.

When you remember your relationships in early-stage addiction, you might be able to see the warning signs of problems that
grew much larger as your addiction progressed.

Relationships in the Middle Stages of Addiction

In the middle stages of addiction, people begin to lose even the illusion of control over the alcohol and the drugs. It becomes more and more obvious that they're using, not because they *want* to, but because they *need* to. It takes more and more to get high, and they start expressing more and more negative consequences of their use. They also start working harder to persuade themselves and others that those consequences aren't their fault and aren't related to the drinking and drugging. Often the blame will fall on their partners.

Common relationship issues in the middle stage of addiction:
- Escalation of control issues
- Issues of denial
- Issues of enabling
- Using the partner as an excuse to drink or use

The Escalation of Control Issues. Rick went through a whole string of romantic partners in the middle stages of his cocaine addiction. His business was failing little by little, he was constantly fighting with his ex-wife and children, and his personal finances were in a disaster. He was attracted to women who were as irresponsible as he was, and somehow he always managed to blame his girlfriends for whatever crises were taking place in his life. They distracted him from his work, they spent his money, they caused tension between him and his children, and on and on. As long as he could blame his partner, he could tell himself that his problems would be solved if he broke up with her. More important, he could avoid looking at what was wrong with his own behavior.

As they feel control over the drug start slipping away, many people start grasping for more control in other areas of life. Relationships are a common target of this need for control. If people tend to say cruel or critical things or use violence against their partners, those behaviors will grow worse during this stage of addiction. Maureen found that, as her addiction progressed, she felt increasingly insecure and needed more of a sense of control over her husband, Ed. Sometimes she would push him away emotionally and criticize him for little things that didn't matter, and at other times she would cling to him and tell him he was too good for her. She kept him just enough off balance to get a sense of power over him, even as she felt more and more powerless in other areas of her life.

> *As they feel control over the drug start slipping away, many people start grasping for more control in other areas of life.*

Denial Issues. People in this stage also lose patience with partners who are honest with them about their inappropriate behavior. Instead, they're drawn to others who will share their denial—other chemically dependent people or codependent people who will protect them from the consequences of their addiction. Dale sacrificed a twenty-year marriage to this stage of his alcoholism. He thought he was having a mid-life crisis when he struck up an affair with a twenty-five-year-old woman who saw him as a brilliant, tortured, misunderstood soul. He felt a little silly when he handed her the old line, "My wife doesn't understand me." The problem was that his wife *did* understand him and had quietly told him that his drinking was putting his job, his marriage, and his life in danger.

> *Addicts in the middle stage are drawn to others who will share their denial—other chemically dependent people or codependents who protect them from the consequences of their addiction.*

Issues of Enabling. In the "safety" of a codependent relationship, the middle-stage addict can drink and use without feeling responsible for the chaos that the addiction is causing. A codependent partner can contribute to this process in many ways. Peter, the overly attentive husband described earlier in this chapter, gives us an example of one method. He cushioned as many of Brittany's self-inflicted blows as possible, taking care of her the way a parent would take care of a little child. When she was too hung over to go to work, he would call in and tell her boss that she had another migraine. When she cried at night and asked him what was wrong with her life, he would tell her that her artistic temperament just made life difficult for her. He tried to help her in every way except the one way that would have helped.

Using the Partner as an Excuse to Drink or Use. Roxanne took another approach to her husband Charlie's addiction. She took on the role of the nagging wife—the same role she had seen her mother take, and the one thing she had said she would never become. She hounded him, criticized him, hid his bottles, and made sarcastic comments as he practically ran out the door to go to the bar. Charlie used to joke with his friends, telling them that he had a little remote control device attached to her face: He could make her raise her left eyebrow just by picking up a bottle. Charlie felt persecuted and never had to look far for an excuse to drink. Still, she paid all the bills, cleaned up his messes, and never even thought about leaving him.

Relationships in the Late Stage of Addiction

In late-stage addiction, systems start to break down much more quickly. At the end, the chemically dependent person's high tolerance for alcohol and drugs is replaced by low tolerance as the body loses its ability to process these substances. This is where the liver, pancreas, brain, and other bodily systems shut down; people lose their last grasp on their dignity; and relationships fall apart under the weight of all that pain. Even strong denial systems sometimes disintegrate, with all the obvious symptoms of addiction staring everyone in the face. Still, in most cases, anyone who tries to stop the addictive process is ignored or driven away.

Common relationship issues in the late stage of addiction:
- Extreme caretaking
- Loss of all relationships in isolation

Extreme Caretaking. The relationships that survive in this stage are the ones based on caretaking. The film *Leaving Las Vegas* gives a vivid portrait of this kind of relationship. In that film, the character of the prostitute Sera took on a role very much like that of a hospice nurse, doing what little she could to protect Ben's pride and keep him comfortable while he drank himself to death.

Loss of All Relationships in Isolation. For most people, though, the end comes in isolation. Very few partners can tolerate the pain of the disintegration that takes place in the final stage of addiction. Chances are you didn't make it to late-stage addiction before you found recovery. More and more people are learning about and trying the option of recovery before they lose everything to the addictive disease. With hard work on yourself, your relationships, and your program—and with help from your recovery network and your other sources of spiritual strength—you'll never have to find out how this stage feels. But if you have progressed to this stage and made it back, you know just how much pain a human being can tolerate.

> *Your relationships won't magically heal just because you're in recovery. They will be just as bad—and even much worse—if you return to drinking or drugging.*

Putting Your Understanding to Use

So now that you've looked at the damage addiction does to relationships, how can you put that information to use? It's important to take stock of what you remember, take responsibility for your part of it, and know that your relationships won't magically heal just because you're in recovery. It's even more important never to forget that it will get just as bad—and even much worse—if you return to drinking or drugging.

If one way to avoid repeating the past is to understand it, another way is to take an active role in building a different future. The next several chapters will help you understand where you are in your recovery and teach you skills that are appropriate for your stage of development. These are skills for finding, building, and caring for healthy relationships. The work you do on your relationships will be some of the most important work you can do to strengthen and hold on to your sobriety.

Chapter 4
The Stages and Tasks of Recovery

When David began to come to terms with being single in recovery, he started looking around for a standard set of rules—a sort of "Ten Commandments for Sober Single People." He didn't find them. What he found was a jumble of stories and advice, many parts of it seeming to cancel out other parts, and all of it raising as many questions as it answered. Why are relationships supposed to be a bad idea during the first year of sobriety? Is it always one year? What if somebody got into a relationship at 360 days? Why do so many marriages break up in sobriety that stood firm during many years of drinking and drugging? Why do so many people with lots of clean time still get into painful and destructive relationships?

In this chapter, you'll find out where you are in the six stages of recovery:

1. Transition
2. Stabilization
3. Early Recovery
4. Middle Recovery
5. Late Recovery
6. Maintenance

The Stages of Recovery

There's no single set of rules on being single and sober, because people's lives, needs, and challenges change as they pass through recovery. Many pieces of advice that are right for someone at three months' sobriety might be all wrong for someone at three years, and vice versa. It's helpful to think about recovery in six stages:

1. **Transition:** Giving up the need to control alcohol and other drug use.

2. **Stabilization:** Recovering from the damage that addictive use caused in your body and your brain.

3. **Early Recovery:** Changing your thoughts, feelings, and actions related to alcohol and drug use (internal changes).

4. **Middle Recovery:** Fixing the damage that addictive use caused in your life and developing a balanced lifestyle (external changes).

5. **Late Recovery:** Growing beyond the limitations imposed by your childhood experiences.

6. **Maintenance:** Balanced living and continued growth and development.

At each stage there are certain **recovery tasks** you need to complete to continue to develop and progress through recovery. People who don't do the work of recovery lead lives that are much more stressful and much less happy. In many cases, failure to do this work ends in relapse.

> *It isn't how quickly you progress through the stages of recovery that matters: it's how completely you do the work that's required of you in each stage.*

At each stage of recovery there are also certain **relationship recovery tasks** you need to complete. Completing these tasks can help you have a happy and satisfying single life and build successful relationships. These tasks are also necessary for your overall growth and recovery. Many people relapse over relationship-related problems that they could have avoided if they knew how to identify and complete their relationship recovery tasks. The next six chapters go into detail on the six stages, their recovery tasks, and the relationship recovery tasks you need to complete in each stage.

Sometimes Quickly, Sometimes Slowly

The stages of recovery might be predictable, but the amount of time you spend in each stage isn't. People pass through the stages of recovery at different rates. That doesn't mean the person who progresses more quickly is smarter, more spiritual, or working a better program. That person might simply have easier challenges to face. It isn't how quickly you progress through the stages of recovery that matters: it's how completely you do the work that's required of you in each stage.

Sue and Clair became friends in treatment, and their friendship deepened as they passed through the early years of recovery. Sometimes Sue would compare herself to Clair, and feel envious and self-conscious because Clair seemed to make so much faster progress in her recovery. Clair lost her compulsion to drink and use early in her program, and Sue was still struggling with strong cravings at ten months. Clair had entered into a peaceful relationship at eight months' sobriety, and Sue was still attracted to abusive men after two years. Clair was making out her eighth-step list (a list of all the people she had harmed) while Sue was writing a very painful fourth step (an inventory of her experiences, strengths, and weaknesses). Sue wondered what was wrong with her that she seemed to be going so slowly.

One day she mentioned her concern to Clair. "Look," said Clair, "If you're going to compare yourself with me, do it a little more thoroughly. Compare the hell you went through as a child with the mild little problems in my family. Compare the two abusive marriages you had before recovery with my little flings. Compare the way your family tries to sabotage your recovery with the help and support I get from my family. Compare your health problems, including chronic depression, with my relatively good health. It's like we're both driving at the same speed, but I'm driving on a flat surface and you're driving over a mountain range.

It's naturally going to look like I'm covering more ground, but I'm not. Comparing ourselves to other people just doesn't work in recovery."

As you read through the next six chapters, don't fall into the trap of comparing yourself with others or kicking yourself for not being farther along in your recovery. As long as you're staying abstinent from alcohol and other drugs, and working on the tasks of your stage of recovery, you're exactly where you should be right now.

Stuck Points

You can also expect to find a few "stuck points" as you progress through recovery. Stuck points are periods of time where you feel trapped in self-defeating thoughts, feelings, and actions. Even though you know these thoughts, feelings, and actions don't promote your recovery or your happiness, you find yourself unwilling or unable to change.

> *It's not whether or not you get stuck that's a sign of success or failure. It's how you cope with the stuck points that counts.*

Tyrone didn't know what the people in his singles recovery group meant when they talked about getting stuck, until the day he realized he was stuck in his fear of being truly intimate. He could have sex, he could talk about his work, he could tell stories about his years of drinking and drugging, but he couldn't talk about how he really felt and the fears that lay deep inside him. Many times he'd made up his mind to try it, but something stopped him every time. He just couldn't force himself to do something that he'd grown up believing would make people laugh at him and stop caring about him. At the next group session he mentioned feeling stuck, and mumbled something about being afraid of talking about his feelings. In their feedback, several of the group members said they had the same fear, and they asked him questions that helped him feel safe opening up a little. As they left for the day, one man came up and shook his hand. "Congratulations," he said. "You've just talked about how you really felt, and survived it!"

It's normal and natural to get stuck once in a while on the road to recovery. It's not whether or not you get stuck that's a sign of success or failure. It's how you cope with the stuck points that counts. If you try to deny or ignore them and slide back into your old ways of coping, you're in trouble. But if you look for help in both new and familiar sources, get the help you need, and accept the fact you're going to have to work harder for a while, a stuck point can be the start of a very productive time in recovery. Chapters four through nine will include some of the more common relationship stuck points and suggest ways of getting past them.

Finding Your Stage of Recovery

Before you look in depth at the six stages of recovery and what they mean to you as a single person, you need to pinpoint the stage of recovery you're in right now. You can do this by answering a series of questions about the stages and reading brief descriptions of the stages and their recovery tasks. The questions will help you get an idea of whether or not you've completed the tasks of each stage. When you get to a stage where one or more of the tasks hasn't been completed, that's the stage where you are now. You'll still need to read about the stages before and after yours, but most of your attention and effort should go into understanding and working on the tasks at this stage.

Before you answer the questions in this section, make a commitment to yourself to try to think about them as thoroughly as you can, and to answer them as honestly as you can. Understanding where you are in the recovery process is very important to the work that you'll do on your life as a single person. You owe it to yourself to get an honest assessment of your stage of recovery.

Stage One: Transition

1. Do you ever see your alcohol or drug use as being caused by other problems in your life?
    ☐ Yes　　☐ No

2. Do you sometimes believe you can solve your problems without total abstinence from alcohol and drugs?
    ☐ Yes　　☐ No

3. Do you sometimes try to control your use of alcohol or drugs by trying to slow down, cut down, only use at certain times of day, use less often, drink or use different substances, or quit for a while?
    ☐ Yes　　☐ No

4. Do you ever believe or tell yourself you can control your use?　　☐ Yes　　☐ No

5. Do you ever believe or tell yourself you're not addicted?　　☐ Yes　　☐ No

6. Do you sometimes believe you can solve your problems without a recovery program?　　☐ Yes　　☐ No

7. Do you ever have doubts about belonging in a recovery program or being willing to follow the advice you get in that program?　　☐ Yes　　☐ No

8. Do you still use any alcohol or other drugs (other than prescribed medication in the prescribed dosage)?
    ☐ Yes　　☐ No

If you answered yes to one or more questions, you're in the transition stage. The major tasks of that stage are recognizing that you've lost control over drinking and drug use, recognizing that you can't control your use because you're addicted, and making a commitment to a program of recovery.

The transition stage starts when your life problems force you to realize you have a problem. At first you might not know your problem has anything to do with alcohol or drugs, so you might try to solve it in all sorts of ways without changing your use of these chemicals. Becky went to three clinical psychologists, a psychiatrist, a hypnotist, and an astrologer before her ongoing problems forced her to look at her drinking patterns. Once she began to admit that she might have a problem with alcohol, she started trying to control her use. She tried quitting forever, quitting for a while, cutting down, slowing down, changing bars, changing drinks, and changing friends. None of it worked.

The major recovery tasks of transition are:

- Recognizing that you've lost control over drinking and drug use
- Recognizing that you've lost control because you're addicted
- Making a commitment to a program of recovery

Finally Becky started paying attention to the information about addiction she had been trying so hard to ignore. She found the courage to approach a coworker who she knew was in recovery to ask her about the signs of addiction. She read some pamphlets. She went to an AA meeting, shaking all the way. She decided it was a nice program, but she wasn't really an alcoholic. She spent another couple of years trying to control her drinking, but kept the phone numbers she'd picked up at the AA meeting.

Becky started having more and more problems at work, problems she could no longer deny were related to her drinking. When she was put on three-months' probation at work, she decided to look for help. Through her Employee Assistance Program she got into a three-day detox and an evening outpatient treatment program. There she learned about the disease of addiction, and slowly came to understand and accept the fact that she really was an alcoholic. After treatment was over, she started going regularly to AA meetings, where she got a sponsor and started to work on the first three steps of AA (admitting powerlessness over her addiction, being open to outside help, and beginning to take the advice of those who could help her). Her decision to make a firm commitment to recovery marked her successful transition. Now she was ready to go into the next stage: stabilization.

Stage Two: Stabilization

1. Are you still shaky or nervous from the last time you stopped using alcohol or drugs?   ☐ Yes   ☐ No

2. When you're under stress, do you ever have a lot of trouble thinking clearly, managing your feelings, avoiding accidents, managing your stress, remembering things, or sleeping restfully?   ☐ Yes   ☐ No

3. When you're under stress or experiencing disappointment or fear, do you sometimes crave alcohol or drugs, or think about how good it was to use and how much it might help if you used again, just this once?
☐ Yes   ☐ No

4. Do you often feel as if your life is insane or unmanageable?   ☐ Yes   ☐ No

5. Do you often feel helpless or hopeless?
☐ Yes   ☐ No

If you answered yes to one or more questions (but didn't qualify for the transition stage), you're in the stabilization stage. The major tasks of stabilization are recovering physically from withdrawal from chemical use, stopping your preoccupation with alcohol and other drugs, learning to solve problems without the use of those substances, and developing hope and motivation to work on recovery.

Once Bruce had made it successfully through detox and made a sincere commitment to work an NA program, he thought the hard part was over. What he didn't expect were the symptoms of **post-acute withdrawal**, a period of six to eighteen months in which the brain works to recover from the damage caused by addictive use. He often felt as if he were in a fog, and when things got stressful, he tended to have a hard time sleeping, thinking and remembering things, and managing his anger and other feelings. He also was physically clumsy at times.

Difficult times—and sometimes even good times—would bring up thoughts about the "good old days" hanging out with his using buddies, and he couldn't seem to turn off those thoughts. When that happened, Bruce went to more meetings, talked to his sponsor about it, and made a first-step list of the problems that using had caused in his life: the experiences that showed him he couldn't control his addiction and that had made his life unmanageable. Even after he'd been clean for five months, he sometimes wondered if he was crazy, or if the program would ever work for him.

The major recovery tasks of stabilization are:
- Recovering physically from withdrawal
- Stopping your preoccupation with alcohol and drugs
- Learning to solve problems without substances
- Developing hope and motivation to work on recovery

Over time, though, Bruce's symptoms started to settle down. He kept showing up at meetings, calling his sponsor, hanging around with other program people, and learning all he could about his addiction. He also joined a problem-solving therapy group to learn how to cope with the pressures of life without using. He came to believe that recovery was possible for him.

Stage Three: Early Recovery

1. Do you ever tell yourself that you're not addicted or that you're different from the other people in your recovery group because your drinking and drugging weren't as bad? ☐ Yes ☐ No

2. Do you sometimes believe your addiction will go away someday and you'll be able to drink and use in ways that won't cause problems in your life?
☐ Yes ☐ No

3. When your "addictive self" and your 'sober self" argue in your head, does the addictive self sometimes seem to be "in charge"? ☐ Yes ☐ No

4. If you're in a 12-Step program, are you still waiting to do your fourth or fifth step, or putting one of those steps off for any reason? ☐ Yes ☐ No

5. Are you still confused about how your addiction affected your life? ☐ Yes ☐ No

6. Are you unsure about the purpose alcohol and drugs served in your life? ☐ Yes ☐ No

7. Do you try to avoid thinking or talking about the past because it's very painful to do so and more comfortable not to? ☐ Yes ☐ No

8. Are you afraid to give a lead (or to share) at self-help group meetings? ☐ Yes ☐ No

If you answered yes to one or more of these questions (but didn't qualify for either of the first two stages), you're in the early recovery stage. The major task of early recovery is to begin to heal your life on the inside. You start that healing by learning to manage and correct the "thinking problem" that makes up a big part of addiction. This includes coming to understand addiction and accept that you're addicted, putting the sober self back in charge of your thinking, understanding the role addiction played in your life, getting to know and understand your life history and your alcohol and drug use history, finding the purpose those substances played in your life, and coming to terms with the pain in your life history. Healing your thinking has a profound effect on your emotions, urges, and actions.

In the first year of recovery, Gail had a spiritual experience she could never explain, but it took away her overpowering urge to drink and use drugs. She was so grateful to have this urge removed and so happy to be clean and sober that she thought the rest of her recovery would be easy. It wasn't. Even though her emotions had stabilized, she often found herself caught up in the "stinking thinking" that people in the program had warned her about. She found herself comparing herself with others in the program, feeling superior, and wondering if she belonged there. It was as if there were a war inside her, with her sober self whispering in her ear and her addictive self shouting it down.

> *The major task of early recovery is to begin to heal your life on the inside.*

Gail was also afraid to think or talk about the things she'd done before recovery, because they were very painful. She was afraid to start writing her fourth step (a personal inventory), even though her sponsor had suggested months ago that she do that step. Finally her sponsor suggested that she keep a journal that would help her see her addictive thinking more clearly. In that journal, Gail recorded conversations that her sober self and her addictive self were having. She wrote about her fears, feelings, and understanding of addiction. She started writing down some scattered memories, then looking into the purposes that her addictive use had served in her life. Before long she was ready to complete her fourth and fifth steps (sharing the fourth-step inventory) and go to work on the sixth and seventh (being willing to give up her self-defeating behaviors).

Stage Four: Middle Recovery

1. Do you ever wonder why you've worked so hard to get sober and stay sober, because there are so many problems in your life?　☐ Yes　☐ No

2. Do you spend a lot of time at your self-help recovery group meetings talking about problems in your life, but find it hard to do what's necessary to solve those problems?　☐ Yes　☐ No

3. Do you tend to put off making changes in your life even though the way things are isn't working for you?
☐ Yes　☐ No

4. If you're in a 12-Step program, have you been putting off doing your eighth and ninth steps (a list of all people you've harmed and the making of amends to them), even though you finished your fifth step a while ago and have been working on the sixth and seventh?
☐ Yes　☐ No

5. Do you tend to eat too much or too little, eat a lot of sweets, drink a lot of coffee or other caffeinated drinks, or get too much or too little exercise?
☐ Yes　☐ No

6. Do you often have "crazy" thoughts, unmanageable feelings, and uncontrollable urges to do things that cause trouble for you or for other people?
☐ Yes　☐ No

7. Do you have a hard time stopping yourself from speaking or acting out of anger, fear, shame, or guilt?
☐ Yes　☐ No

8. Do you have a hard time communicating openly and honestly with the people you love?
☐ Yes　☐ No

> 9. Are there problems in your friendships, romantic rela-
> tionships, family relationships, or relationships with the
> people at work?   ☐ Yes   ☐ No
>
> 10. Do you have a hard time handling the ups and downs
> of life without chemicals?   ☐ Yes   ☐ No

If you answered yes to one or more of these questions (but
didn't qualify for any of the first three stages), you're in the
middle recovery stage. If early recovery focuses on internal
change and healing, middle recovery focuses on healing the outer
world and building a balanced lifestyle. The major focus is on repairing the damage that addiction has done to your life and relationships. Recovery tasks include working on solutions to the
problems in your life that cause pain and upset; trying to make
up for the damage your addiction has done to other people; setting up and following a program of physical health and balance;
learning to manage your thoughts, feelings, urges, and actions; and
learning to act and communicate in healthy ways in all your relationships.

> *Middle recovery focuses on healing the outer*
> *world and building a balanced lifestyle. The*
> *major focus is on repairing the damage that*
> *addiction has done to your life and relationships.*

A lot of people in Eddie's AA and NA groups looked up to him.
He was very much committed to the Twelve Steps, went to a lot
of meetings, gave wonderful comments, and sponsored several
men. But Eddie's life was a mess. He was overweight, he drank
too much coffee and smoked too many cigarettes, he worked com-
pulsively, he lost his temper too often, and he never seemed to
be able to be faithful in his romantic relationships. Eddie believed
he was ready to do his eighth and ninth steps (a list of the people

he'd harmed and an attempt to repair the damage), but something kept stopping him. He finally had to admit that he hadn't been able to do those steps because he hadn't made much progress in the sixth and seventh steps. He understood the program and knew how to "talk the talk," but except for his abstinence from alcohol and drugs, he wasn't really "walking the walk." He needed to work on changing his behavior in the present, so he could make amends for the past without fear of repeating it.

Stage Five: Late Recovery

1. Did you grow up in a family where one or more members was chemically dependent?　☐ Yes　☐ No

2. Did you grow up in a family troubled by mental illness, violence or sexual abuse, inability to express feelings, poverty or low income, divorce, the death of a parent or sibling, or frequent conflict?　☐ Yes　☐ No

3. Do your thoughts often drown out your feelings, or your feelings often drown out your thoughts?
☐ Yes　☐ No

4. Do you try to avoid or cover up unpleasant feelings by ignoring those feelings, "stuffing" them inside you, focusing on other people's needs and mistakes, blaming others for your problems, clowning, or acting out with inappropriate behavior?　☐ Yes　☐ No

5. Are there large parts of your childhood that you can't remember?　☐ Yes　☐ No

6. Do unpleasant memories sometimes come back to you very forcefully, raising a lot of fear and pain?
☐ Yes　☐ No

7. Do you tend to be involved with romantic partners who hurt you in ways similar to the ways that authority figures treated you in childhood?　☐ Yes　☐ No

---

8. Do you tend to have a hard time solving problems or changing your behavior when you know you need to change? ☐ Yes ☐ No

9. Do you tend to try to make peace, rescue other people from their pain, blame yourself for other people's problems, or do what others want you to do even though you don't want to do it? ☐ Yes ☐ No

If you answered yes to one or more of these questions (but didn't qualify for any of the first four stages), you're in the late recovery stage. Not everyone has to go through this stage, because not everyone was raised in troubled or *dysfunctional* families. Healthy families teach children to cope with life effectively. If these children become addicted in later life, they have an easier time in recovery, because they aren't carrying around a lot of unhealed wounds from childhood.

The major recovery tasks of late recovery are:

- Recognizing your childhood issues
- Getting accurate information about your family of origin
- Mapping out your childhood history
- Understanding the connection between your childhood and problems as an adult
- Changing your adult lifestyle to reflect the healing of childhood wounds

On the other hand, people who were raised in dysfunctional families often learned to survive and cope with life in ways that cause problems in adulthood. These problems are sometimes called **psychotherapeutic issues** because they often have to be dealt with in therapy. These issues weren't caused by the addiction, and simply getting sober doesn't heal them. Psychotherapeutic issues often come out most dramatically and most painfully in romantic relationships.

The tasks of late recovery include recognizing your childhood issues, getting accurate information about your **family of origin** (the family you grew up in), mapping out your childhood history, understanding the connection between your childhood problems and your problems as an adult, and changing your adult lifestyle to reflect the healing of childhood wounds.

Richard and Denise loved each other very much, but it often seemed that the smallest issues would get blown up into major conflicts and sources of pain for both partners. When Richard was upset, his actions would remind Denise of her overbearing alcoholic father. Her reactions would remind Richard of his anxious, dependent mother. Each one tended to react to the other one's behavior by slipping automatically into the behaviors that had helped him or her survive as a child, but those behaviors made things much worse in the relationship. Even though they worked good recovery programs, Denise and Richard needed both couples counseling and individual counseling to learn different ways of being with one another.

Stage Six: Maintenance

1. Do you often find that your peace of mind is stronger than your fear of the future and your shame or guilt over the past?   ☐ Yes   ☐ No

2. Do you find that you can usually keep your serenity with little disturbance even when things are going wrong in your life?   ☐ Yes   ☐ No

3. Are you usually able to focus on your own responsibilities—stay on your own side of the street—instead of worrying about what other people are doing wrong?
☐ Yes   ☐ No

---

4. When you find yourself slipping into the old addictive ways of thinking, managing your feelings, and acting on them, are you usually willing and able to find and accept the help you need to get back on track?
☐ Yes ☐ No

5. Do you usually treat your body and your mind well, getting the proper food and exercise?
☐ Yes ☐ No

6. Are you usually able to operate without the dysfunctional coping styles left over from childhood?
☐ Yes ☐ No

7. If you have a current or recent relationship, is it a happy one, where you're not replaying any of the old roles or painful feelings from your childhood?
☐ Yes ☐ No

If you answered yes to all of these questions, you're in the maintenance stage. The major focus of this stage is on protecting the hard work you've done in recovery and continuing to improve your lifestyle. Recovery tasks include keeping up an ongoing recovery program, coping with day-to-day problems in constructive ways, working on ongoing personal growth, coping with changes and complications in life, and coping with stuck points in recovery. This is the stage where the "promises" on pages 83 and 84 of the "Big Book" (*Alcoholics Anonymous*) come true and stay true. That doesn't mean you won't get stuck in the old thoughts, feelings, and actions once in a while. Under stress, you might even experience symptoms of post-acute withdrawal from time to time. But you'll use all the tools at your disposal to cope with those problems and continue to make even more progress in your ongoing growth and healing.

> **The major recovery tasks of maintenance are:**
>
> - Keeping up an ongoing recovery program
> - Coping with day-to-day problems in constructive ways
> - Working on ongoing personal growth
> - Coping with changes and complications in life
> - Coping with stuck points of recovery

Carol is a longtime AA member who has been through a lot of pain and growth in sobriety. She still has her difficult days, but in general she's peaceful and happy. The tenth, eleventh, and twelfth steps are a regular part of her life (taking daily self-inventory, working on her spirituality, carrying the message to others, and practicing recovery principles in her daily life). She's quick to admit her mistakes and take responsibility for solving any problems she's caused. She has a strong sense of meaning and purpose in life, and she stays involved in AA to help others and continue to work on her own personal growth.

Carol's two most recent relationships were happy ones that ended without anger or bitterness, and right now she's enjoying being single. She recently went through successful radiation and chemotherapy for cancer. Through that process, she never hesitated to accept the emotional support she needed from the many people who love her. But she never stopped feeling spiritually connected and grateful for her sober years.

Completing the Tasks of Each Stage

As you've completed these checklists and read through these stage descriptions, you probably found that some elements of more than one stage were true for you. That's normal. But keep in mind that to do the work of one stage effectively, you need to have completed all the work in the stage before it. Don't try to skip a stage or breeze through it because you think the next stage is more important. If you do, the unfinished business from the earlier stage can get in the way of your progress in the later one. And skipping any of these tasks can lead to relapse.

In the next six chapters, you'll see a lot more information about how the challenges and recovery tasks of each stage affect your relationships and your relationship recovery tasks. This will give you not a set of rules, but a sort of treasure map to help guide you through the obstacles and danger zones in each stage. The treasure at the end is you: someone who can stay sober and be happy and productive, in or out of relationships.

> *To do the work of one stage effectively, you need*
> *to have completed all the tasks of the stage before*
> *it. Skipping any of these tasks can lead to relapse.*

Chapter 5

Transition

This chapter is about being single in the transition stage of recovery. The transition stage begins when you start to wonder if you might have some kind of problem, and ends when you commit to a program of recovery from chemical dependency. If you're in the transition stage right now, you might be abstinent from alcohol and drugs, or you might still be using. You might feel clear-headed, or you might be completely confused and unable to focus on the words on this page. You might be feeling calm right now, or you might be jumping out of your skin.

In this chapter, you'll look at:

- One man's transition story
- An overview of the transition stage
- The relationship recovery tasks of transition
- The core questions in the transition stage
- Single time in transition
- Being in relationships in the transition stage
- A relationship recovery agenda
- Hope for recovery

Whatever state of mind you're in right now is the state of mind you're in. If reading this book is confusing or upsetting to you, that probably means you're not ready to read it yet. If reading this book calms you down and gives you a feeling of hope, that probably means you need to read it now. You might desperately need to understand more about relationships and being single in order to get through the transition stage. Or you might desperately need to ignore relationships and being single right now and just focus on not picking up a drink or a drug. If you're not sure, try reading and see if you feel more or less hopeful about recovery. Ask your counselor. Read one small section at a time, or one paragraph at a time. Do whatever seems to strengthen your hope and commitment to recovery.

A Transition Story

When Mark went through treatment the first time, he did it for Julie. They were engaged at the time, and Julie had told Mark he would have to stop drinking or she wouldn't marry him. He loved her very much and had been desperately lonely since she left. He had come to the conclusion that he was nothing by himself and needed her to survive. The only way to get her back would be to show her that he was willing to do something about his drinking and drug use. In treatment, Mark couldn't identify with a lot of the things people said, and he didn't really believe he was chemically dependent. But he did and said what the counselors wanted him to do and say, and never mentioned his doubts. Instead, he analyzed everything they told him, arguing with them only in his head.

After he finished treatment Mark started going to AA and CA meetings. He showed up late and left early, and got away from anyone who seemed to want to talk to him. He used all his will power to keep from drinking or using, but his life was still miserable. That proved to him that the alcohol and drugs weren't his main problem. His main problem was that nobody loved him, and Julie had abandoned him. After a month had passed, he called Julie and told her he'd been sober for a month and he was going to 12-Step meetings. She was very happy for him, told him she'd never stopped loving him, and agreed to start seeing him again.

After they'd been going out together for a couple of months, Mark stopped going to meetings. He decided it would be OK to drink and smoke pot every once in a while, as long as he didn't do it in front of Julie. After all, he wasn't a real addict. He'd only been drinking and using too much because he'd felt Julie slipping away from him. Now that she was back and sure that she loved him, he wouldn't drink or use anywhere near as much as he did before. But it took only two weeks to get back to his regular pattern of use, and Julie soon figured out what was going on. When Julie left for the second time, Mark held onto his bottle and his pipe for dear life. It took another six months for him to admit that he really had a problem, and that his problem was addiction. He entered detox again, ready to make—and keep—a commitment to recovery for his own sake.

An Overview of the Transition Stage

This phase of Mark's life is a good example of what happens in the transition stage. He knew he had a problem, but before he could find its true cause, he had to look everywhere else for an explanation. As you may remember from chapter four, the major recovery tasks of transition are:

1. recognizing you've lost control over drinking and drug use;
2. recognizing you've lost control because you're addicted; and
3. making a commitment to a program of recovery.

If you're in the transition stage, you're probably not sure whether you're addicted and need to be abstinent from alcohol and other drugs. You may find yourself questioning everything people tell you about addiction and exploring the consequences of trying to control your use. Like Mark, you might see more differences than similarities between your life and the lives of the people you meet in recovery programs.

Transition is a time for testing and questioning. How else can you be sure of your commitment to recovery, if you decide to make one? For a successful transition, you need as much accurate information as possible. Anyone or anything that helps you get accurate information is going to help you in this stage. You might find all kinds of ways of denying that information, but after a while there might be too much information to deny. Anyone or anything that keeps you from getting accurate information—or strengthens your denial—is going to work against you in this stage.

In transition, the people you have in your life can be helpful or harmful, depending on whether or not they go along with your denial.

In our example, Julie was very helpful to Mark. When she left him the first time, her leaving told him that his drinking and drugging were unacceptable to her. The pain he felt after she left forced him to try treatment as a desperate measure to get her back. When she came back to him after he said he was in recovery, he had a chance to test his theory about not really being addicted. He stopped going to meetings, experimented with controlled use, and learned that he couldn't control his use, even though he had Julie back in his life. When he lost her again, he was forced to look at himself. What he saw made him commit to a program of recovery.

In the transition stage, the way you conduct your life and the people you have in your life can be helpful or harmful, depending on how they affect your search for information about your addiction, and whether or not they go along with your denial. Julie could have protected Mark from the consequences of his use by taking care of him or sticking with him no matter what he did. But if she had, it would have taken much longer for him to find out what was really wrong in his life. He might have died trying. And Mark, when he was in treatment the first time and in self-help meetings afterward, could have helped himself by being honest about his doubts. Instead, he pretended to understand and agree with what he heard. He carried his doubts with him into another ten months' worth of drinking and using.

The Relationship Recovery Tasks of Transition

As if the addiction-recovery tasks weren't tough enough, each stage also has its own relationship recovery tasks. These tasks are necessary, not only for the health and happiness of your relationships but also to avoid relationship-related relapse.

The relationship recovery tasks of transition:

- Stop using relationships and partners as an excuse for getting high
- Get to the real cause of your problems—your addiction
- See how the addiction affects the relationship
- Make conscious choices about whether or not to keep using
- Make conscious choices about the relationship
- Intervene on actively addicted partners
- Get some distance from addicted or enabling relationships

In transition you need to stop using relationships as an excuse for getting high, and stop letting your partners use you as an excuse to get high. Instead, you both need to get to the true cause of the problems. So far relationships have been handy tools for "defocusing" from the addiction—taking your attention away from what's going on inside you—or making excuses for your drinking and drug use. Often people who are actively addicted say things like, "If your [boyfriend/girlfriend/husband/wife] were like mine, you'd drink too!" This shows a backwards cause-and-effect reasoning: "I drink or drug because I have relationship problems."

Instead, the truth is, "I have relationship problems *because* I drink or drug."

> *In the transition stage there's a strong temptation to fall in love with someone who has significantly more recovery than you, as if that relationship would increase your comfort and security in recovery.*

During the transition stage the focus of the relationship must be on intervention. This means you need to see the real cause-and-effect relationship. You need to make conscious choices about whether or not you're going to continue to drink or use drugs, and whether or not you're going to stay in the relationship. If you're in a relationship with an active addict, now is the time to intervene. Ask your partner to get help for his or her addiction; if your partner continues in active addiction, you need to get enough distance to keep yourself safe from exposure to these substances. If you're an addict whose partner is enabling your addiction, you also need to get some distance from that relationship in order to get well.

It's also important to note one of the dangers related to the transition stage. Many recovering people in the late stage of recovery have relationships with newly recovering people and get pulled into a codependent style of relationship—trying to "fix" or cure the new person with all the tools they've gained in the program. In the transition stage there's a strong temptation to fall in love with someone who has significantly more recovery than you, as if that relationship would increase your comfort and security in recovery. But if that person has not dealt with his or her codependency issues—and many people with long-term sobriety have not—then he or she may well want to take care of you and solve your problems for you. Your partner's responses can create pain and problems that are relapse triggers for you. It's far better to avoid relationships in this stage.

Core Questions in the Transition Stage

Being single in the transition stage can be helpful or harmful. It depends on your beliefs about being single and on the way you spend your time. It's important to explore your relationship with being single. Remember the core questions mentioned in chapter one ("If I'm single, will I always be alone?" "What do I have to offer?" and "Am I unlovable?"). If you're in the transition stage, think about your answers to those questions *as they feel to you right now*. If they're being honest, many people in the transition stage tend to answer those questions in fairly negative ways. It makes sense: their lives are falling apart, and hope is hard to find. Quite often their addiction has destroyed relationships, and they've spent time in relationships that nearly destroyed them. If you're battling feelings of shame and self-hatred, it's going to be hard to believe that you're worthwhile all by yourself.

Using the Core Questions as Weapons

Justine used the negative answers to these questions as weapons against herself and against the hope of recovery. Her logic went this way: "If I'll always be alone, then the pain will be unbearable, so I need to medicate it with booze and drugs. If I have nothing to offer to others, then I have nothing to lose by destroying myself. And if I'm unlovable and undesirable, I'm doomed to a life of repeated abandonment."

> *As you build your recovery program, you'll have more to offer to others and to yourself. The strengths you'll build will make you more lovable and desirable than you can imagine.*

The trouble with that logic is that it's based on false statements. When Justine found recovery, she learned that being single didn't mean she would always be alone. In or out of a relationship, if you take part in a fellowship of recovery, you'll never have to be alone again. As you build your recovery program, you'll have more and more to offer to others and to yourself. And the courage, strength, and compassion you'll build will make you more lovable and desirable than you can imagine now.

Using the Core Questions to Heal

If you do decide to make a firm commitment to recovery, you can follow this book through the next five stages of recovery. At each stage you'll have a chance to answer the core questions again as you experience them at that stage. You'll be amazed at how your answers to the core questions can change as you grow and heal.

As a single person, you might at this moment be in a relationship, you might be between relationships, or you might have chosen to stay single. Being out of relationships—what we call "single time"—is a completely different experience from being in a relationship, even if that relationship doesn't last very long. Each of those states can affect your sobriety positively or negatively. The next couple of sections look at how this works in the transition stage.

Single Time in the Transition Stage

It's important to look at how you use your single time in this stage—the purposes it serves in your life. This has been divided into two categories: Using single time to feed the disease of addiction, and using single time to feed recovery. Feeding the disease includes all the unhealthy purposes that being out of relationships can fulfill, the ones that move you closer to drinking and drugging. Feeding recovery includes the healthy purposes, the ones that move you closer to ongoing sobriety and emotional health.

Using Single Time to Feed the Disease

We said earlier that the basic need in the transition stage is for accurate information about addiction and about the effects of your chemical use. It makes sense that you would starve your recovery and feed the disease by using your single time to block out that information. As long as Wendy didn't want to stop drinking, she was in some ways more comfortable being alone most of the time. She could distract herself from her feelings of loneliness and live in isolation. Nobody noticed or commented on how much she was drinking. Nobody tried to stop her. Nobody challenged her denial about her addiction. Nobody drank her liquor before she could get to it. Nobody showed her what her addictive drinking could do to a partner.

Even the loneliness she felt helped her keep drinking. It became the excuse to drink, proof that she was worthless. If she had answered the core questions about being single, she would have said, "Of course, I'll always be alone. I have nothing to offer. I'm terminally unlovable and undesirable." Wendy's isolation was a dark cave that she crawled into to lick her wounds. As long as no one else saw her shame, she could pretend she wasn't feeling it. A partner might have turned a light on her problem and shown her some truths that she wasn't ready to face.

Thought and Discussion Questions

1. In the transition stage, what are (or were) three ways you blocked out or medicated your loneliness with alcohol or drugs?
2. How did your use of those substances block out your feelings about being single?
3. At this point in your recovery, what do you believe is the difference between feeling alone and feeling lonely?

Using Single Time to Feed Recovery

Not being in a relationship might be an excuse for addictive isolation, but it doesn't have to be. It can be the best opportunity to carve out a safe place to heal. When Wendy started to take her addiction seriously, she started using her single time in a more constructive way. Instead of seeing it as a way to keep people from messing with her drinking, she started looking at it as a way to keep people from messing with her recovery. Maybe there was nobody at home to challenge her denial, but there was also nobody there to strengthen her denial by protecting her from the consequences of her actions.

Using single time to feed the disease:

No one:
- sees or comments on how much you're using
- tries to stop you or get you to accept help
- shares your supply
- shows you what your addictive use can do to a partner

Loneliness and isolation become the best excuse to drink and use.

Using single time to feed recovery:

No one has a stake in enabling your addiction.
There's time to develop recovering friends, who:
- help you begin to build a sober social life
- go out for coffee and talk about recovery principles
- are available for support when you're feeling shaky

Solitude becomes a quiet place to seek spiritual strength and guidance.

Wendy found that she bonded with AA people much more quickly and deeply because she was free to go to as many meetings as she wanted, then go out for coffee with women who had been in the program for a while. She also spent a lot of time on the phone with program people. She grew closer to them because there was no primary partner competing for her attention. The alone time that used to feel like isolation now felt like solitude—a quiet place where she could calm her spirit and seek higher guidance. Her single state no longer kept her from getting accurate information about her addiction. Now it helped her get more information, from more sources.

Thought and Discussion Questions

1. What is the most important action you can take to get through the transition stage and make healthy decisions about your addiction?
2. What are two positive ways you can get input from people with solid sobriety during the transition stage?

Being in a Relationship in the Transition Stage

Many people are already in relationships when they enter the transition stage. While in some cases it would help the recovery process if those relationships weren't there, it wouldn't be practical to suggest that everyone break off their relationships at this stage. Some of these relationships are promising ones that might survive the early stages of recovery and help you along the way. Others might not survive the early stages, but they might be necessary to get you through the transition stage. Still others are self-destructive and harmful to recovery, but you might not be able to let go of them yet, even though you know it would be best.

Your preexisting relationship:
- Might survive the early stages of recovery and grow into a healthy relationship
- Might not survive too long, but it will help you get through transition
- Might be a self-destructive relationship that will hurt your recovery in the long run
- Might be so destructive that you need to get out of it now

You need to be honest with yourself about which kind of relationship it is.

If you're in the transition stage and you're thinking of starting a new relationship or going back to an old relationship that has already ended, please think again. This wouldn't be a good time to start a relationship. For one thing, as confused as you are right now, you're likely to choose the wrong partner. And even if you choose the right partner, with all the pain and changes you're going through, you're likely to mess up the relationship. But an even more important danger is that new relationships tend to pull your energy and attention away from recovery and lead you into several more years' worth of misery. If this is the right partner for you, he or she will wait until you're more stable. If this isn't the right partner, why put your recovery at risk?

Thought and Discussion Questions

1. If you're in the transition stage and you're already in a relationship, would you describe that relationship as: (a) supportive of your recovery, (b) fairly supportive of your recovery, or (c) not supportive of your recovery? Please explain.

2. If a good friend of yours was in the transition stage and was thinking about starting a new relationship, what is the most important thing you would tell him or her?

Using Relationships to Feed the Disease

Being in a relationship can be a handy way of blocking accurate information about the effects of your addiction. All of us tend to find people who will fill certain roles in our lives, healthy or unhealthy. We also find subtle ways of "training" people to fill the roles we think we need, although we're usually not aware that we need those roles or that we're fitting people into them. These people might be sexual or romantic partners, but any person who has a close relationship can fill one or more of these roles. Here are some of the roles that feed the disease by blocking out valuable information about your addiction. Some of them will be familiar from the stories told in earlier chapters.

Stool Pigeon: Someone you can blame for the problems in your life, so you won't have to look at what you're doing to cause or contribute to those problems. Charlie was convinced that his drinking was due to his wife Roxanne's nagging, so he didn't even think about other causes.

Villain: Someone who abuses or picks on you, so you can feel like a victim and not feel responsible for what you do. Gwen always seemed to get into relationships with sarcastic men who criticized her every move. All her attention and energy went into thoughts of how mean they were to her, and how helpless she was.

Protector: Someone who protects you from the consequences of your addiction, so you won't have to feel the pain that would lead you to look at what you're doing. Peter had Brittany so well protected that she never needed to question her drinking patterns.

We find subtle ways of "training" people to fill the roles we think we need, although we're usually not aware that we need those roles or that we're fitting people into them.

Gatekeeper: Someone who keeps you from doing things that will hurt you, so you won't feel the consequences and you won't have to learn to protect yourself. Myra's husband was always in charge of the bottle and did all the ordering in restaurants. It was only after his death that she began to drink all she wanted, and soon she was drinking all day, every day.

Worst-Case Scenario: Someone whose addictive behaviors are so bad that you can compare yourself with that person and look good. Joe knew he wasn't an alcoholic because he was so much better off than his business partner.

Sole Supporter: Someone on whom you can focus all your trust and loyalty, so you can shut out all the other people who might be honest with you about your addiction. Karin and Renee were best friends, supporting one another through everything.

Anyone who said anything against either of them—especially about Karin's drug use—was an enemy to both of them.

Savior: Someone you can identify as your last and only chance for happiness and emotional survival. This way you won't have to look at recovery as a source of hope, and you'll have an excuse to fail if you lose this person. Mark was convinced that he would die without Julie, and when she left him he had all the reason he needed to sink into worse and worse addictive use.

It's not just in the transition stage that chemically dependent people tend to assign these roles to partners. These roles can also cause problems in later stages of recovery. In those stages it's usually not drinking or drug use that's being masked by these roles, but some other kind of self-defeating behavior.

Thought and Discussion Questions

1. If you have (or had) a partner in the transition stage, which of these roles do you think you might have assigned to your partner, and why? Please explain.
2. What is the most important thing you learned about yourself in your relationship with this type of person?

Using Relationships to Feed Recovery

If you've identified a current partner who's playing some of those unhealthy roles, you might be feeling pretty discouraged. Please don't give up. Even if you choose to stay with your partner, you can assign different roles that promote your recovery.

One sad truth in life is that we can't change other people. We can work on changing ourselves—our ways of managing our thoughts, feelings, and actions—and we can have great success at that. When we do change ourselves, it often changes our attitudes about other people. We no longer need them to fill those old roles, so we start seeing them in different roles. When Charlie started working an AA program, he had to stop blaming Roxanne for his drinking. After a while, he started seeing her as just another imperfect human being who had a habit of nagging him. He stopped taking it personally. That took a lot of his anger away.

Unhealthy Roles for People in Your Life	Transformed into Healthy Roles
Stool Pigeon	*Imperfect Being*
Takes all the blame	Simply makes mistakes
Villain	*Runaway Train*
Makes you a helpless victim	Somebody to be cautious about
Protector	*Supporter*
Keeps you from feeling your pain	Gives you emotional support
Gatekeeper	*Teacher*
Keeps you from getting in trouble	Example of self-discipline
Worst-Case Scenario	*Coming Attraction*
Makes you look good by comparison	Shows you where you might end up
Sole Supporter	*Team Member*
The only one on your side	One of many on your side
Savior	*Asset*
Your only hope for happiness	Someone you enjoy having in your life

Changing our behavior can also change the shape of our relationships, and the partner who was comfortable in the old relationship may not be comfortable in the new one. Roxanne was happy that Charlie had stopped drinking, but after years of taking the role of the nag, she found that she didn't know how to relate to the new Charlie. She also had a lot of anger left over from his years of irresponsibility. She started finding new things to complain about and reminding him of all the years he spent drunk. But instead of slinking off to the bar, he stood there and nodded, not looking guilty at all. Their marriage was about to fall apart when a friend gently steered her to Al-Anon.

What happened? Charlie transformed the role Roxanne was playing for him. She used to be the scapegoat, the one he blamed for his drinking. He transformed her role into that of just another imperfect human being who was sometimes a pain in the butt. He stopped getting mad, stopped running away from her, stopped playing the push-and-pull game they'd been playing for years. And when she kept pushing and he didn't pull, she didn't know what to do.

Some partners will be willing and able to change to fit their new roles in your life, but some won't. You won't know until you change your own life, for your own sake. Getting clean and sober might mean risking the loss of a partner who, for whatever reason, needs to have you actively addicted in order to feel OK. Saving your life is worth risking the loss of that partner. There are plenty of places your partner can get help, if he or she chooses.

Here are the old roles, transformed so that they feed recovery instead of feeding the disease:

Imperfect Being: The old stool pigeon, turned into just another person who makes mistakes.

Runaway Train: The old villain, someone who tends to abuse you or put you down. When you stop playing the victim and start taking responsibility for your life, the villain loses a lot of his or her power. But you still need to respect the fact that this person is a source of danger. If you're in a physically abusive relationship, you'll need the help of a domestic violence counselor as soon as possible, to decide how to handle it. Even if the abuse isn't physical, you'll need counseling, group therapy, a relationship recovery group, and/or a skilled sponsor.

Supporter: You can learn to see the old protector as a source of genuine support—not to protect you from the consequences of your addiction, but to give you emotional support as you go through the difficult early days of recovery. Usually the enabler will need help from Al Anon, Codependents Anonymous, or private counseling in order to make this shift. In any case, it's important that you stop accepting enabling behaviors from your partner. If that's not possible, you might need to get some distance during the first few months of recovery.

Teacher: Often the old gatekeeper is someone who has a lot of self-discipline. You can learn to admire and follow this person's example of self-discipline while you stop letting him or her control your life. Again, sometimes your partner will need to get help from Al-Anon or another source, or you'll need to get some distance until you're stronger.

Coming Attraction: This is the old worst-case scenario who used to serve as evidence you weren't sick, because he or she was so much sicker. In recovery you can learn to see this person with compassion, but with your eyes wide open. It's important never to forget what active addiction can do to human lives.

Team Member: He or she used to be your sole supporter—your only ally against the world. In recovery you'll need many people helping and supporting you, and this person can be invited to be an important part of your support network. He or she might need help in making the change, or you might need to get some distance until you're stronger.

Asset: The partner who used to be your savior can't fill that role anymore as you find many new sources of hope in your life. But that partner can be a good part of your life—a source of love, joy, pleasure, and gratitude. When you let your partner off the hook as your only hope, only then can you start to discover who he or she really is.

A Relationship Recovery Agenda

If you're in the transition stage, here are steps you can take toward relationship recovery. These steps will help you move toward healthy recovery and toward healthy relationships.

1. Accept that you're in a state of change and not sure what you want or need to do about your chemical use. Make a list of all the conflicts that are keeping you from either being satisfied with your chemical use, or keeping a commitment to recovery. What would be the advantages and disadvantages of using alcohol or drugs to cope with these conflicts?

2. Think about how you use relationship problems—or the absence of a relationship in your life—as an excuse for drinking or drugging. Make a list of all the ways you do this. Now make another list of all the ways your drinking or drugging might be causing problems in your relationships.

3. Think about how your partner's actions might be making it easier for you to drink or use, and harder for you to get help. How does your partner make excuses for you, overlook your drug-affected mistakes, make those substances more available to you, or cover up for you?

4. Start to communicate honestly with the people close to you about your confusion and need for support in this process. Identify at least two people who can support you in this process.

5. Get some input from sober people and from others who understand chemical dependency. What is the first step you need to take to get this input?

6. Learn to recognize the attitudes and behaviors in the people close to you that tend to feed your disease: Who are the people in your life who tend to feed your disease? What are the attitudes and behaviors in those people that tend to feed your disease?

7. If people you care about are feeding your disease, ask them to get help for themselves. What words would you be comfortable using to ask the people you care about to get help for themselves? How will you feel, and what action can you take, if they say no?

8. If people can't or won't get help for themselves, get some distance from them until you're stronger. What steps would you be comfortable taking to get some distance from people who can't or won't get help for themselves?

9. Identify the people in your life who feed your recovery by being honest with you, giving you hope, and encouraging healthy choices in your life. Name at least two people in your life who feed your recovery.

10. Start to increase the recovery-feeding influences in your life by spending more time around these people or having more communication with them. What steps might you take to increase the recovery-feeding influences in your life?

11. Accept the fact that your success in relationships will depend on your success in recovery. What evidence have you seen that the effects of addiction tend to hurt relationships?

12. Make a commitment to recovery, for your own sake. What steps might you take to make and keep this commitment?

Hope

You've just taken in a lot of information in this chapter. If you're in the transition stage, it's possible that much of it won't make sense to you. That's OK. You can understand very little and still get through the transition stage successfully, as long as you understand just three things: (1) Drinking and drugging don't work for you anymore because you're addicted; (2) there is hope for you; and (3) to get your life back on track, you'll need to accept help.

As you move through the stages of recovery, there will be plenty of time to think about relationships and roles, who you are and who your partner is. If working on it now helps, then this is the time to start working on it. You can read ahead to the other chapters—a sort of preview of coming attractions—or you can read this chapter more than once and really learn what it has to teach. If thinking about it makes your head spin, put this book down and pick it up in a month or so.

The most important thing is that you get the help you need and find the hope you deserve.

Chapter
6

Stabilization

Jeannie was discouraged. It was her fourth try at sobriety, and she was doubting her ability to recover. She'd never made it past eight or nine months before, even though she'd been thoroughly committed to the idea of recovery. She'd gone to meetings, read the Big Book, gone out for coffee, called her sponsor—at least at first. Something always went wrong in those first few months.

In this chapter, you'll look at:
- Challenges during stabilization
- Relationship recovery tasks in stabilization
- Being single in stabilization
- Relationships in the stabilization stage
- Relationship risks to stabilization
- Putting recovery first

Now that she was trying it again, she remembered what had gone wrong. It had been three months since her last episode of drinking and drugging, and tonight she was still jumping out of her skin. She'd just had another argument with her boss today, and she was afraid she was going to lose her job. She couldn't sleep, think straight, or understand her emotions. She was afraid to even try to go to sleep because of the horrible dreams she'd been having. They were nightmares, bringing back long-forgotten memories of abuse by her uncle. She knew she couldn't drink anymore, but she really wanted to smoke a joint right now. She told herself that wouldn't be quite as bad as drinking.

Jeannie felt so lonely and unprotected that she was about to go out of her mind, and there was a message from Robert on her voice mail. Her sponsor had suggested that she stay away from relationships, but if she just got together with him for coffee or a late dinner, that wouldn't be a relationship. Besides, Robert was new in the program, too, so it would just be two newcomers giving one another support. Her sponsor would never have to know.

Challenges during Stabilization

What Jeannie didn't know was that she was experiencing some challenges that are very common during the stabilization stage, the phase that begins when you've made a commitment to a program of recovery.

Major challenges during stabilization:
- Post-acute withdrawal
- Post-traumatic stress disorder
- Cravings and addictive thinking
- Euphoric recall

Post-Acute Withdrawal

One condition Jeannie was experiencing is post-acute withdrawal (PAW), a set of symptoms that come up after people finish the three-to-ten-day detoxification process. PAW is the outward sign that the brain is trying to heal from all the poison that's been pumped into it. PAW can create difficulty with thinking clearly, managing feelings, avoiding accidents, managing stress, remembering things, or sleeping restfully. Some people have mild PAW symptoms, and others have strong ones. The symptoms last anywhere from six to eighteen months. In the stabilization stage, people's lives are often still in turmoil from the crises that pushed them into recovery. PAW symptoms can stir up that turmoil even more and make life quite difficult.

There are a number of things you can do to calm the PAW symptoms and simply "ride them out" without letting them do much damage. One is to follow a healthy diet and exercise plan from a doctor who understands your condition. Avoid sugar and caffeine, because they really stir up the PAW symptoms and interfere with sleep. Nicotine can cause problems, too. If you're an addicted smoker, you probably won't be able to cut down. You're better off stopping smoking at the same time you stop all other substances, so you can detoxify from them all at once. This is particularly true if you're in an inpatient setting.

It's important to go to a lot of meetings, spend time with sober people, and try not to think about things you can't do anything about right now. Doing "ninety in ninety"—attending a meeting a day for the first three months of sobriety—is an excellent idea, especially if you have strong PAW symptoms. You might want to get some therapy or training in relaxation and stress-management skills, because PAW symptoms grow worse when you're under stress. And if you have strong PAW symptoms, you might also need relapse prevention therapy.

Thought and Discussion Questions
1. PAW symptoms include difficulty with thinking clearly, managing feelings, avoiding accidents, managing stress, remembering things, and sleeping restfully. Which of these symptoms do (or did) you have in the stabilization stage of your recovery?
2. What kinds of thoughts or life events bring out these symptoms in you?
3. What steps might you take to calm these symptoms and protect your recovery?

Post-Traumatic Stress Disorder
Jeannie was also having symptoms of post-traumatic stress disorder (PTSD). As mentioned briefly in the first chapter, PTSD is

a condition that comes from the way the brain protects us from painful and frightening experiences that we can't cope with emotionally. This often happens in cases of child abuse, rape, battering, violence in the community, or combat in times of war. Often the brain "represses" or hides the feelings and memories from those situations—like Jennie's brain hid the abuse by her uncle—until it's safe to remember them. When those memories come up, they sometimes come in nightmares or in intense waking memories called "flashbacks." Other PTSD symptoms include loss of sleep, being jumpy or easily startled (called "hypervigilance"), depression, numbness, anger, and fear.

Alcohol and other drugs help push the feelings and memories under. Unfortunately, when those substances are removed, the memories and other symptoms of PTSD often start to surface. This happens even though the stabilization stage is not a particularly safe time to deal with them because of all the life crises and PAW symptoms that are taking place. But once the memories and feelings have come up, you can't successfully shove them back under, and you can only do damage if you try. At that point you need to get professional help in managing the PTSD symptoms—as soon as possible.

> *Once the memories and feelings have come up, you can't successfully shove them back under, and you can only do damage if you try. You need professional help in managing the PTSD.*

If you do have PTSD, and if well-meaning friends in the program tell you not to try to deal with childhood issues during the first year, don't take them seriously. They probably don't have PTSD, so they won't understand what you're going through. However, during this stage it's important that you choose a therapist who's willing to just help you cope with the memories and feelings that you *do* have. Neither you nor your therapist should try to look for any more lost memories. If there's anything in your past that you don't remember, you've forgotten it for good reasons. Leave it alone at this stage of recovery. Be aware, though, that these memories will come back at some point. When they do, you'll need to work through them with the help and support of a therapist who knows how to treat PTSD.

Thought and Discussion Questions

1. The symptoms of PTSD include nightmares, flashbacks, loss of sleep, hypervigilance, depression, numbness, anger, and fear. Do you have any of these symptoms? If so, which ones?
2. If you have symptoms of PTSD, what steps can you take to get the professional help you need?

Cravings and Addictive Thinking

Jeannie knew from past experience that her cravings for alcohol and drugs wouldn't go away if she used, but she told herself that if she only used a little, it might put the cravings to sleep. Then she told herself that calling Robert was the best and only way to keep herself from drinking or using that night. Cravings are a common and serious problem for most people in the stabilization stage. So is the addictive thinking that lies to them about what would happen if they drank, used, or did other things that tend to lead to more problems, and so to more cravings.

> *The best way to fight euphoric recall is to follow the pleasant memory all the way to its unpleasant end, including the pain of detox. Run the whole movie through again before you decide to buy another ticket.*

Euphoric Recall

An important part of addictive thinking is euphoric recall. Euphoric recall is the mind's tendency to remember only the pleasant parts of experiences that often led to pain. Jeannie often remembered the pleasure of the first few joints, the first few drinks, the first line of cocaine, laughing with using friends, and dancing in bars. She forgot the sickness in the morning, the jagged edge of coming down, and the humiliation of waking up with men she would never have slept with if they didn't have drugs. When she thought of Robert, she remembered only the excitement of new relationships and forgot the anguish of fighting, breaking up, and going down the relapse spiral.

The best way to fight euphoric recall is to follow the pleasant memory all the way to its unpleasant end. Don't leave anything out. For every first drink or drug, there's all the pain that leads to detox, the pain of detox, and the defeat of coming back and saying "I blew it"—if you're one of the lucky few who make it back. Run the whole movie through again before you decide to buy another ticket.

When cravings show up, it's important to remember two things: (1) If you give in to the craving by drinking or using, the craving might go away for a while, but it will come back much worse; and (2) if you don't give in to the craving, but instead call someone who has solid recovery and talk about how you feel, the craving will eventually get tired and go away. If you don't give in to this craving, the next one will be a little easier to deal with.

Thought and Discussion Questions

1. When you get into euphoric recall, what kinds of memories are strongest in your mind?
2. What kinds of experiences are you conveniently forgetting when you get into euphoric recall?

3. List three healthy people you can call who can help if you get cravings, even in the middle of the night (don't list people you'd like to be involved with sexually, or people who seem to be interested in you that way). If you don't have three people right now, find them in your meetings.
4. What would be a good way of starting the conversation if you call one of those people?

Life crises, PAW, PTSD symptoms, cravings, and addictive thinking can give the stabilization stage all the force of a hurricane. As you can imagine, this hurricane can destroy sobriety, careers, and relationships. Your job is to do all you can to promote the healing you need and to get through this stage without drinking, drugging, or doing anything else that will hurt you or others.

When you have cravings, remember:

If you give in to the craving, it will come back much worse.

If you don't give in, but instead call someone with solid recovery:

- the craving will eventually go away, and
- the next one will be a little easier to deal with.

The major tasks of this stage are recovering physically from withdrawal, stopping your preoccupation with alcohol and drugs, learning to solve problems without drinking or using, and building hope and motivation to work on recovery. How hard you'll have to work on those tasks depends on how much chaos remains in your life, how severe your PAW symptoms and cravings are, and whether or not you have PTSD symptoms coming up at this time.

Relationship Recovery Tasks in Stabilization

In stabilization, the primary addiction-recovery task is to recover from acute and post-acute withdrawal and resolve the current crises in your life. The relationship recovery tasks support that overall goal. Often during stabilization, people feel torn between focusing on recovery and focusing on the relationship. The choices you make will be important. You need to *stop* defocusing your attention away from your life and onto the relationship, and *start* paying attention to the problems you need to solve in order to stay sober.

Relationship recovery tasks in stabilization:

- Take the focus of your attention away from your relationship.
- Put your primary focus on your recovery, and keep it there.
- Find relationships that will help you keep recovery first.
- Encourage your partner to get help for him- or herself.
- Negotiate a supportive, low-intensity relationship.

You need to find relationships that will support your need to put recovery first. You need to give yourself time to get well. If you're in a relationship, both partners should get into recovery. If your partner is not addicted to alcohol or other drugs, then he or she might find some help in programs like Al-Anon, Nar-Anon, or Coc-Anon. As a couple, you need to take some time out to negotiate a mutually supportive relationship, but one that operates on a much lower level of stress and intensity. *Remember:* Anything that distracts you from your recovery is dangerous. If you gamble your sobriety on your relationship, you'll probably end up losing both.

Being Single in Stabilization

As in the transition stage, single time can seem like a blessing or a curse in stabilization, depending on how you look at it and use it. Think again about the three core questions of being single ("Will I always be alone?" "What do I have to offer?" and "Am I unlovable?").

The confused thoughts and extreme emotions of the stabilization stage can easily distort the answers to these questions and turn them into weapons people use to attack themselves and their recovery. In the case of Jeannie described above, she had many people in her life who cared about her quite a bit. But she had a lot of pain in her life because of what was going on in her brain. And she had a lot of sexual desire, because she was human and spending her evenings in meetings with men who were attractive to her. She put all that together and said: "I'm lonely."

> *In stabilization, people often want to get into relationships to ease their pain—the problem is that they've never had time to understand why they experienced pain in past relationships.*

Keeping Issues Separate

Jeannie wasn't really lonely. She was horny, and she was in emotional pain. She was also scared of her answers to the core questions: "If I can't get recovery, and if my life's always going to be a mess, what could I possibly offer in a relationship? Will I always feel alone like this?" She didn't know how to separate horniness from loneliness, being alone from being lonely, being single from being unlovable, or being single now from being single for the rest of her life. She could have dealt with those things one at a time—taken care of her own sexual needs, called a few friends to get rid of the loneliness, and told herself that the rest of her life was none of her business right now. But instead she lumped them all together, so she couldn't begin to cope with them.

Escaping into Relationships

In a hurricane, people often cling to the nearest tree, even if it isn't strong enough to stand against the wind. In the stabilization phase, people often want to get into relationships as a way to ease their pain—never mind that they've never had time to understand all the pain they've experienced in past relationships. Sometimes even the same partners who trashed them before, and are still out there drinking and drugging, look like a source of relief.

To Jeannie, the call from Robert sounded like her one desperate hope. She told herself she wouldn't get involved with him, even as she threw a condom into her purse, "just in case." So far she had done everything exactly as she'd done it her first three times in recovery. She had always ended up isolating with her new boyfriend, skipping meetings, not calling her sponsor out of guilt, and eventually getting back to the drink and the drug.

But the next day, she did something differently. She called her sponsor and told her about her night with Robert. She expected an angry lecture—even wondered if her sponsor would "fire" her—based on the ways her past sponsors had reacted when she finally told them she was in a relationship. But this sponsor was different. "OK," she said, after a moment's silence. "Last night is part of the past. Let's work on a plan to get you through this time safely. Stick with me. We'll get through it." Jeannie felt hope for the first time she could remember.

Judgment Problems in Stabilization

In the stabilization stage, most people are all wrong about the people or circumstances that would make them happy in the long run of their lives. The most dangerous people often appear to be the most attractive. You don't even know who you are right now, much less who would be right for you. Your brain is doing all it can to heal from its chemical poisons. It's simply not ready to handle the larger life questions like, "Will I find a lasting relationship?" or "Do I even want a relationship?" The stabilization stage is time to let go of those kinds of questions and trust that they'll be answered in time. Just try to keep your mind on the little day-to-day things that will keep you sober and move you toward greater peace of mind.

Thought and Discussion Questions

1. What do you think is the difference between being lonely and being horny?
2. What are some ways of taking care of horniness without finding a partner?
3. Describe the loneliest part of being single.
4. What are two new and different positive actions you can take when you feel lonely?
5. Describe the positive qualities of another single person (not a potential romantic interest) whom you would describe as lovable and desirable.
6. How can you use single time to strengthen your recovery?

Saying No to Relationships

If you're currently not involved in a relationship, staying out of relationships for a while might be the most important thing you can do to protect your recovery. But how do you do that?

Many people in our society, addicted or not, believe they don't have a right to disappoint others, even if their own well-being depends on it. Char thought she couldn't turn a guy down for a date unless she already had a boyfriend—or pretended she did. Now in sobriety, she had no boyfriend and she was trying to be honest, so she had no more excuses. She believed she had to go out with Todd, especially since he was saying it wasn't really a date.

> *Many people in our society, addicted or not,*
> *believe they don't have a right to disappoint others,*
> *even if their own well-being depends on it.*

Knowing Char's relationship history, her sponsor was a bit alarmed. First she reminded Char that disappointing someone was not the same thing as hurting him. Then she worked with Char for an hour, and together they came up with a list of possible things she could say to him. Then they did a role play, with her sponsor playing the role of a disappointed Todd.

Char: My sponsor has suggested that I stick with women in the program for a while, and I've decided to follow her advice. I'm really sorry, but I'm going to have to cancel for tomorrow night.

Todd: Oh, don't tell me. No relationships for the first year. I told you, this isn't a date, and it certainly isn't a relationship. I just want to get together for coffee, talk about the steps or something.

Char: I know it's not really a date, but my mind has a hard time telling the difference, so I'm going to have to say no. I hope you understand.

Todd: No, I don't. Is it something about me that you don't like?

Char: It's got nothing to do with you. But my mind is really made up.

Todd: Sounds like your mind is playing games on you.

Char: You have a right to your opinion. I'm going to have to go now.

By the time they'd rehearsed it three different ways, Char felt confident calling Todd to cancel. As it turned out, he wasn't upset and backed off easily. But she would have been prepared even if he'd given her a lot of trouble.

Thought and Discussion Questions

1. What are two things you would feel comfortable saying to someone who appears to want to get to know you in a romantic way, if you think it might be dangerous for you?
2. What might you say if this person refused to understand what you were saying?
3. What might you say if this person got mad?
4. Name two people who would be willing to role-play this conversation with you, so you can feel prepared if the situation comes up.

Even if you're not sure getting involved would be dangerous for you right now, please try to say no, at least until you understand why it would be dangerous. But if you do get involved, don't hide it. Tell somebody you can trust to be honest and accepting of you. Tell your sponsor, and if your sponsor blows up at you, find someone else with good sobriety and talk to him or her about it. Many people in this stage have relapsed because they got involved in romantic or sexual relationships. But many of those people could have made it through if they had talked about it with someone who could help them stay on track in their recovery.

Relationships in the Stabilization Stage

In the stabilization stage, recovery has to come first. Anything that takes your energy and attention away from recovery might threaten your very survival. So what can you do if you're already in a relationship? If your life is still in crisis because of the aftereffects of active addiction, your relationship may be in crisis, too. Stabilizing your body and brain is hard enough. How do you stabilize your relationships? How do you keep recovery first when your relationship is demanding your time and attention?

Setting Up a Recovery Structure

Whether or not you're involved with anyone, the first step is to set up a strong structure of recovery activities. This should include regular meetings, including a home group that you attend every week, and "ninety in ninety" if you have strong PAW symptoms; a sponsor, whom you call on a regular basis; a call-list of recovering people, whom you call regularly even when you're not in crisis; regular exercise and a healthy diet; therapy, if you have PTSD symptoms or strong PAW symptoms; and quiet time for reflection, meditation, and spiritual communication.

> *Stabilizing your body and brain is hard enough. How do you stabilize your relationships? How do you keep recovery first when your relationship is demanding your time and attention?*

Getting Your Partner's Support

If you're in a relationship, your partner needs to know about and accept your whole recovery program. If your partner is also willing to get into a program of recovery like Al-Anon, Nar-Anon, CODA (Codependents Anonymous), etc., it will help your partner, your relationship, and your own recovery. If you can safely draw your partner into your new life by going to open meetings together and going out to dinner with other recovering people, this will also be good for both of you, and for the relationship.

Thought and Discussion Questions

1. What elements of your recovery program do you follow on a regular (daily or weekly) basis?
2. What elements do you think you should add to your recovery program to get you safely through the stabilization stage?

126

3. If you're in a relationship, does your partner have a recovery program? If so, please describe it. If not, what obstacles keep your partner from having a program?
4. If you were to ask your partner to do something more to support your recovery, what would that be, and what words would you use to ask?

Relationship Risks to Stabilization

If relationships were always peaceful, they wouldn't hold so many risks for newly recovering people. But all relationships have trouble and conflict, and the relationships that chemically dependent people get into tend to have more trouble and conflict than most. With any relationship, it's important that you look at it honestly to see how it might affect your recovery. Here are a few relationship conditions that can complicate the stabilization stage.

Relationship risks to stabilization:

- Conflict out of control
- Your partner's needs and jealousy
- Active addiction and abuse

Conflict Out of Control

Most people don't have the skills to fight fairly and honorably. Their hurt and anger are fueled by deep fears that they don't fully know or understand. They strike out in anger, in a blind impulse to return the pain. Of course, alcohol and drug abuse make this worse. These chemicals lower people's ability to think about the consequences of their words and actions and hold back the really damaging blows. They also give people more problems to fight about.

In the stabilization stage, many people's emotions are raw. Their wounds are close to the surface. In their closest relationships, they may be caught up in cycles of uncontrollable fighting. When Art went into treatment, it seemed like his one chance to save his stormy relationship with Dorie. But when he came out of treatment, the fight started again as if it had never stopped. There was so much hurt on both sides that no one knew who was reacting to what. Each one saw only the pain that the other had inflicted, and saw his or her reactions as necessary and justified.

It took a double session with Art's counselor to start the couple on the road to peace. They began lessons in stress and conflict management techniques, and they set up a structure for putting down the battle and establishing new patterns of communication. They had to let go of the idea of blame entirely and work on understanding each other. It was hard, but it saved the relationship *and* Art's sobriety.

Thought and Discussion Questions

1. If you're in a relationship now, identify the biggest conflict in that relationship?
2. How does this conflict affect your stability in recovery?
3. What are some steps you might take to improve your conflict management skills?

Partners' Needs and Jealousy

Sometimes even the most supportive partners find themselves having trouble when their partners get sober and start working a program of recovery.

> **You'll need to be aware of your partner's needs and problems, which might include:**
>
> - Your partner's desire for a social partner in drinking situations
> - Jealousy of your sober friends and people at meetings
> - Fear of losing your loyalty or love
> - Your partner's need for emotional support

Desire for a Social Partner. Jack couldn't have been a better cheerleader for Nan's recovery. He took her to detox and her first treatment session, gave her pep talk after pep talk, and held her when she cried through the early days. But Jack's work required that he do a lot of entertaining, and he didn't know how to be the perfect host without his longtime hostess. Once Nan had stabilized enough to look and sound good, he was back with all the invitations to parties and out to dinner with friends. He didn't seem to understand her fear of those kinds of situations, and he promised that he'd take care of her. She felt great loyalty to Jack, but she knew that for every invitation she accepted she was skipping a meeting and putting herself in the presence of a lot of alcohol. With the help of her sponsor, she finally sat down with him and explained what she needed to do to stay sober. She had to stop playing hostess and start spending her evenings at meetings.

Being Jealous of Sober Friends. For Warren, the situation was even more tense. He could tell that his girlfriend Jackie was jealous of his new life, but she wouldn't come out and say it. Every once in a while she'd smile and make some flip comment about "those cute little bimbos" at his NA meetings. And if he stayed too long after meetings talking to people, she'd sulk when he got home and refuse to tell him what was wrong. He was afraid to make any female friends in the program, and even afraid to spend much time with his sponsor and his male friends. When he suggested that she go to Nar-Anon, she just patted his head and laughed.

Fear of Losing You. Jackie's feelings ran much deeper than simple jealousy. She was deeply frightened of the new life he had, a life that didn't include her. She'd never had much confidence, but as long as he was weakened by active addiction, she could tell herself he couldn't do any better than her. She'd never learned to confront her fears or talk about them honestly. All she could do was strike out with a quick joke and retreat into silence. After three months of this hit-and-run conflict, Warren had to tell Jackie that he was about to make one of three choices: relapse, break off the relationship, or get into couples counseling. After a long and tearful fight, she agreed to try couples counseling.

> *Without the attention and support of a recovery program, your partner might have an even harder time adjusting to sober life than you do.*

Your Partner's Need for Support. As hard as your life is right now, your partner's life might be difficult, too. Without the attention and support of a recovery program, your partner might have an even harder time adjusting to sober life than you do. If your partner was with you through worst days of your addiction, he or she might be full of anger and resentment that it just wasn't possible to express before. If you give your recovery all the energy and attention that you need to give, your partner might feel left out and unimportant, as if he or she had been thrown away with your painful past.

Active Addiction and Abuse

If your partner is still drinking or using regularly or addictively, the relationship can be dangerous to your recovery. It can trigger euphoric recall, feelings of nostalgia for the "good old days," and cravings. Every time Nan would watch Jack and his buddies tie one on, she would feel left out. She couldn't help remembering how much better it felt to be lifting a glass with them in the old days. Her cravings would rise up so strong that she didn't think she could stand it. And even though Jack had promised to watch her like a hawk, she knew she'd find herself alone again later, and the cravings would still be there.

Abuse from Addicted Partners. In some cases your partner might also be cruel or abusive to you—emotionally, sexually, or physically. People who could cope with abuse while they were still drinking and drugging usually find the abuse much more painful in sobriety. In the stabilization stage, with so many sources of pain and confusion, abuse from a partner can be intolerable.

131

If your partner is still drinking or using, the relationship can be dangerous to your recovery. It can trigger euphoric recall, feelings of nostalgia for the "good old days," and cravings.

Sara thought she could take anything from her boyfriend, as long as she could medicate her pain with alcohol and drugs. But when she got clean, the memories and feelings started rising so strongly that she thought she'd go crazy or kill herself if she didn't go back to using. She finally moved out in the middle of the night and went to a domestic violence shelter. There were many times during the first few months when she wanted to go back to him, and it took all her strength to stop herself. Now, at three years' sobriety, she's glad she did what she did.

Thought and Discussion Questions

1. If your partner still drinks or uses regularly or addictively, what elements of that situation are the most difficult or stressful for you?
2. What effect does your partner's use appear to be having on your recovery right now?
3. What effect might your partner's use have if you stay in the relationship?
4. What steps might you take to keep your recovery safe?
5. Does your partner do or say anything that you would describe as cruel or abusive? Please explain.
6. What effect does this behavior have on your recovery now?
7. What effect might this behavior have if the relationship stays the same or gets worse?
8. What steps might you take to keep your recovery safe?

Putting Recovery First

Surviving the stabilization stage is both an art and a science. It's an art because no one can explain all the little miracles that happen in recovery. It's a science because you need to learn to observe yourself, as if from outside. Allow whatever crazy thoughts and emotions come to you at this stage. But at the same time, watch what's happening in your head, and say, "That's interesting. I reacted to that person's comment by feeling very angry. I wonder what that's all about." You don't need to find all the answers, and you won't. It's enough just to be aware, and to ask the questions. Keeping a journal—and reading it from time to time—can be very helpful in this process.

Spotting Destructive Relationships

In the same way, you need to become a good observer of your feelings and attitudes about being single, and of the way partners or possible partners appear to affect your recovery. A person can be very good, intelligent, and strong, and still have a destructive effect on your sobriety. Nate never did understand why his relationship with Cora made him skip meetings and feel cynical about recovery. She was a fine woman and very supportive. But he watched himself carefully, keeping track of the time he spent with her and the effort he put toward his program. He finally had to admit that there was a problem and put the relationship down for a while.

Why put your recovery first?

- Your partner can be a wonderful person and still harm your sobriety.
- If a relationship is hurting one partner, it's not helping the other one either.
- If you do what's necessary to get and stay healthy, it will help your partner, too, in the long run.
- If you don't put your recovery first, you're likely to relapse.

Doing What You Need to Do

If you love your partner—or if you feel like you need your partner for emotional or financial support—it might seem selfish to put your recovery needs ahead of your partner's wishes. But please remember this: If a relationship is hurting one partner, then it's not helping the other one either. It's not even helping the partner who appears to be running the show and getting what he or she wants.

If you do what's necessary to get yourself strong and healthy, it will not hurt your partner, even if it disappoints your partner or makes him or her angry. It might even help, even if the relationship falls away and your partner hits bottom on his or her problems. If you need the help of a therapist to do it, it's worth getting that help, no matter how much it costs. With the proper help, you will get through it. Letting go of a destructive relationship will not destroy either partner. It might be both people's only hope.

Thought and Discussion Questions

1. Think of an incident lately when you lost your temper or got carried away with difficult emotions. If you were watching yourself from the sidelines at the time, what might you have said about your thoughts, feelings, and actions?
2. If you're in a relationship now, what would the "objective observer" in you say about your partner's effects on your recovery?
3. What steps do you think you should take to strengthen your recovery?

Chapter 7

Early Recovery

From the first time Beth walked into Rob's Tuesday night NA meeting, Rob's comments changed. The change wasn't even subtle, but Rob didn't seem to notice it. The person he had been when he was "out there" changed from a troubled guy struggling with alcohol and cocaine abuse, into a high-rolling heavy hitter on the nightclub scene. Instead of the few times he'd gone into bad neighborhoods to buy cocaine for friends, he turned into a pistol-packing mega-dealer who knew no fear. And the few hollow-eyed girls who sometimes hung around for coke were transformed into gorgeous supermodels who hung on his arms and followed him everywhere.

In this chapter, you'll look at:
- Relationship recovery tasks in early recovery
- Being single in early recovery
- Identifying high-risk partners
- Learning to listen
- Building a sober social network

One night after the meeting Rob walked into the rest room and was startled to see himself in the mirror instead of Antonio Banderas. What the hell was he doing? Did he think this would impress Beth? Had she said anything to give him the impression that she was that phony? He'd always thought he was an honest person, but now he was coming head-to-head with one of the many ways his addictive self could take over in sobriety.

Relationship Recovery Tasks in Early Recovery

Addressing those kinds of addictive thinking patterns is one of the purposes of early recovery, a slightly more peaceful time than stabilization, with plenty of opportunities for learning. The major goal of this stage is to change the attitudes and beliefs that often set people up to relapse. In this stage you explore and correct the "thinking problem" behind the "drinking problem." Tasks at this stage include: coming to understand addiction and accept the fact that you're addicted; putting your sober self in charge of your thinking; understanding the role addiction played in your life; getting to know your life history and the history of your alcohol and drug use; finding the purposes those substances played in your life; and coming to terms with the pain in your life history.

In other words, early recovery is all about seeing and accepting the truth and learning to be honest. It's no coincidence that the first paragraph of "How It Works" (an explanation of recovery principles read at each AA meeting) uses the word "honest" three times. Without honesty, you have *little* chance of staying sober and *no* chance of building healthy relationships or a healthy single life.

Relationship recovery tasks in early recovery:

- Recognizing addictive thoughts, feelings, and actions connected with relationships
- Recognizing high-risk partners and high-risk relationships
- Saying no to these relationships, or getting out of them
- Being open to low-risk relationships

In early recovery, you learn to make clear distinctions between your old addictive and irresponsible thoughts, feelings, and actions and the sober and responsible thoughts, feelings, and actions that you want to cultivate. If this is confusing to you, please don't feel alone: *Most addicted people don't know the difference.*

Reducing the Risk in Your Relationships

Unfortunately, there are many addictive thoughts, feelings, and actions associated with relationships. Early recovery is a time to learn to recognize high-risk addictive partners and high-risk addictive relationships. It's also a time to learn how to say no to these relationships, or to get out before the relationships blow up and jeopardize your recovery. And finally, it's a time to learn to accept low-risk, safe, loving relationships. You may have noticed these kinds of relationships before, and you may have dismissed them as "boring." In active addiction, many people learn to equate intensity, risk, and danger with love. When they find themselves in a truly safe relationship, they believe nothing's going on because they don't feel the intensity and fear.

Continuing Recovery Tasks from Earlier Stages

Much of the work you started in the transition and stabilization stages will have to continue now. If a friend or family member is still doing things to enable your addictive behavior, you'll need to take your responsibilities back and encourage the enabler to get help. You'll still need to work on your stress level so that the PAW symptoms don't come back to haunt you. You'll need to continue to manage any PTSD symptoms, cravings, and addictive thinking. You'll have to continue to work on your feelings and attitudes about being single. And if you're in a relationship, you'll need to continue to work on the relationship and monitor your partner's effects on your recovery. It will be best for both of you if your partner stays involved in an ongoing recovery program, whether that's Al-Anon or another 12-Step program, therapy, or another kind of self-help group.

Along with the many tasks of chemical dependency recovery in this stage, there are also recovery tasks related to being single and being with people. These include coming to terms with who you are right now as a single and sober person, learning to listen, and learning to build a sober social network. These skills will help you stay safe and build a foundation for healthy relationships—including a healthier relationship with yourself.

Being Single in Early Recovery

In early recovery, many single people become impatient with all the open questions in their lives. It's like recovery from a broken leg: After the intense pain is over, it starts itching under the cast. Many people wonder why they haven't found "The One," or why the relationships they've started have turned out to be so painful.

The truth is that you're supposed to be confused at this stage of your recovery, and you're supposed to be making mistakes in your judgment of others and yourself. That's because your addictive self is still in charge some of the time. You haven't yet developed the overriding sense of honesty with yourself that is the subject of this stage's work. Being honest is more than just not telling lies on purpose. For example, Ron thought he was a totally honest person until a friend asked him why he'd been avoiding her. He realized that he'd been angry and playing games, unwilling to take a chance and admit that something she'd said had hurt him.

Relationship Dangers in Early Recovery

In this stage you're still in danger of sinking into isolation, or jumping into unhealthy relationships. It's not so long since you ended an important relationship with mood-altering chemicals. Many of your actions are really reactions to the loss of that relationship. The temptation to distract yourself from the pain of real life, and from the reality of who you are, can be great. Relationships—even painful ones—make effective distractions. You're probably not going to want to hear this, but in early recovery it's still too early to safely start new relationships. This is the time to build the basic social skills that you missed when you were out drinking and drugging.

> *Early recovery is an excellent time to build the basic social skills that human beings are meant to develop before they get sexually or romantically involved.*

Making Up for Lost Development

By now you may have learned that people's basic social and emotional development stops at the point when they begin using alcohol and other drugs. If you were abused as a child, or exposed to much violence in your community, parts of your development might have stopped at the time the abuse or violence started, even if you hadn't yet started drinking or using. In recovery, you have a chance to work through the developmental stages you missed as a child, an adolescent, and an adult. It's hard, but you're surrounded by others who are also making up for lost growth.

For that reason, early recovery is an excellent time to build the basic social skills that human beings are meant to develop before they get sexually or romantically involved. A big part of that process is coming to understand what you need and want, and becoming aware of the types of people who are dangerous for you. The next step is to develop social networks that give you the companionship and support you need. Only then will you be able to approach relationships from a position of strength and balance.

> *In recovery, you'll have many opportunities for friendship with good people who are working hard to get well. Don't undervalue those people just because you're not sexually attracted to them right now.*

Alone, Lonely, or Horny?

Your attitudes toward single time might also start changing as you move through early recovery. Where once it might have been impossible to see the difference between not being in a committed partnership right now and being alone forever, you might now start to accept your single time as temporary and necessary. Whether or not a lifelong committed partnership is waiting for you is a question you still don't have enough information to answer. When Jody was in early recovery, one day she came to the conclusion that it was OK not to know what was in store for her. And even if it *wasn't* OK not to know, that wouldn't change the fact that she simply didn't and couldn't know at the time. She had to let go of the questions.

You also might be starting to accept the difference between being lonely and having unsatisfied sexual desires. As the saying goes, "It's easier to get through times of love and no sex than it is to get through times of sex and no love." If you're giving full attention to your new life and your recovery program, you have many opportunities for friendship with good people who are working hard to get well and stay sober. It's important not to undervalue those people just because you're not sexually attracted to them.

Thought and Discussion Questions

1. In sobriety, have there been any changes in your feelings about single time vs. being alone? Please explain.
2. What are two ways sobriety has affected your feelings about your sexuality?
3. What kinds of things (events, times of day, day of the week, etc.) tend to trigger feelings of loneliness in you?
4. What are some self-defeating things that you tend to do when you're alone?
5. What are some steps you can take to cope with feelings of loneliness in healthier ways?
6. What obstacles could prevent you from taking these steps?
7. What steps might you take to overcome those obstacles?

Learning to Grieve

When Diane got past the stabilization stage, she was surprised to find that she was still crying far too often about her divorce. After all, it had taken place six years before she entered recovery. Wasn't she done with it yet? Through her therapist she learned that the effects of addictive chemical use make it impossible to grieve a loss completely and effectively. Alcohol and drugs are often used to medicate the pain of loss. At the time, there may be a lot of crying and depression—even dramatic scenes. But the most important work of grieving isn't taking place. After people get sober they often find themselves grieving losses they thought were long resolved. This is normal and natural.

The process of grieving is much more than just crying and talking about people or experiences you've lost. Grieving includes many emotions, from denial, numbness, and depression to anxiety, anger, fear, and sadness. The fact that you need to grieve a loss doesn't mean you're weak in any way. All human beings need to grieve their losses. If they pretend nothing is wrong and just "keep a stiff upper lip," the pain just goes inward and causes illness or compulsive behavior.

There are many ways of grieving and many phases that are part of the grieving process. If you've suffered a loss, it's important to acknowledge that loss and let yourself feel whatever you feel. But it's also important to share those feelings with others who care about you and understand your loss. Many recovery groups are excellent places to be when you're grieving, because others have suffered losses, too, and because it's OK to express your emotions.

Your losses might include broken relationships; partners, relatives, or friends who died while you were in active addiction; the loss of children to divorce or foster care; the loss of careers to the effects of addiction; the loss of important abilities to illness or injury; or any number of troubles that people live through. In each case, it also involves the loss of some of your dreams about what your life would be like with this person, this job, this ability, etc. As you grieve your losses, you're also grieving the loss of your dreams.

> *After people get sober they often find themselves*
> *grieving losses they thought were long resolved.*
> *This is normal and natural.*

In therapy and through sober friends, Diane learned that her grief wouldn't last forever, although she found that idea hard to believe. Her sad memories would fade, and her happy memories would live on in a way she could handle. Over time, her lost dreams would be replaced by the new dreams she was building in sobriety. If she worked her program well, these new dreams would be based on the truth, instead of the illusions that had led to her marriage, but eventually destroyed it.

Thought and Discussion Questions

1. In recovery, what are the losses that come back from your past to cause you pain? Please explain.
2. In your own words, define or describe "grieving."
3. Name two people or places you can go to for help in grieving those losses.

Identifying High-Risk People

Your experience with alcohol and drugs has probably taught you that those substances aren't good for you and that they'll eventually cause you trouble and pain. In the same way, there are probably certain types of people who aren't good for you, and eventually they'll cause you trouble and pain. Many of these might be people you're attracted to as sexual or romantic partners. Others might be potential friends. As you start to build your sober social skills and networks, it's important to pinpoint the types of people who are bad news for you. If a friend or lover tends to raise your stress or lower your mood, energy, or confidence, that person might also endanger your sobriety. It might feel good now to be with him or her, but it will feel much worse later.

Clues from Past Relationships

You'll find important clues about these "high-risk people" in your own life history. If you're in a 12-Step program, in this stage you might be approaching or completing your fourth and fifth steps (an inventory of your life experiences and your strengths, weaknesses, and motivation; and the sharing of that inventory with another person). High-risk people might play a part in that process, or they might rate a little fourth step of their own. Here's what Andy learned about his high-risk romantic partner.

When he thought about the women who had really put him through the ringer, Andy remembered that he'd always fallen for them very hard and very quickly. They were exciting to him. They drank and used too much, but that was OK with him at the time. He always felt a little off balance with them. They treated him differently at different times, sometimes lovingly and sometimes angrily. They often led him to believe they would be his forever, then told him they needed more space for a while. At first they cried a lot about the way other people were treating them, until he hated those other people. Then, over time, he became the one who was treating them badly. And it was true. He tried to do everything for them, but by the end he was losing his temper regularly. He hated himself around them.

> *If someone raises your stress or lowers your mood, energy, or confidence, that person might also endanger your sobriety. It might feel good now, but it will feel much worse later.*

At first he had told himself that he'd left that kind of woman behind with the drinking and the drugs, but now he wasn't sure. He was attracted to a woman he saw at meetings, and he'd thought about asking her out, but she reminded him a little bit of a couple of his old girlfriends. His sponsor suggested that he write down a description of his high-risk partners, their relationships, and how he had let himself be pulled into involvement with them. When he finished that description, Andy decided not to ask the woman out right away, but to listen to her comments for a while and see if there was any resemblance. The night she ranted and raved about how mean her boss was—at a meeting where they were supposed to be talking about taking personal responsibility—he decided not to ask her out.

Thought and Discussion Questions

1. Think of one type of person who has meant trouble for you in the past. It can be a type of partner, friend, etc. You can use qualities from more than one person.
2. What qualities most strongly attracted you to that type of person?
3. What seemed most comfortable or familiar about your relationship with that person?
4. How did that person tend to treat you throughout the relationship?
5. How did you tend to treat that person throughout the relationship?
6. How did you feel about yourself around that person when the relationship was going well?
7. How did you feel about yourself around that person when the relationship wasn't going well?
8. What was your main expectation of your partner in that relationship?
9. Was it realistic to have that expectation of that person at the time? Why or why not?
10. What was your partner's main expectation of you in that relationship?
11. Was it realistic to have that expectation of you at the time? Why or why not?

12. What role did alcohol and drug use play in that relationship?
13. Was it most often you or your partner who ended your relationships?
14. How did you feel when those relationships ended?
15. What did you do to cope with those feelings?
16. Who in your present life is like that person in some important ways? Describe the similarities.
17. What steps might you take to keep from repeating your old relationship patterns with this person?

Learning to Listen

Another good preparation for sober social life is some training in listening skills. Most people are so focused on how they come across when they talk that they forget the importance of listening. Effective listening is much more than just hearing the words the other person is saying. We need to give those words our full attention, instead of judging the person who's speaking, or preparing our answers so we can jump right in when the speaker pauses for a second. Then we need to make sure we understood what was said.

Active listening skills:
- Listen to what your partner says.
- "What I hear you saying is.... Have I got that right?"
- Listen to your partner's answer.
- Give your honest reaction.

Vern thought Rita was going to be *the* woman for his first sober relationship—until the night she slammed the phone down in his ear. What had happened? He didn't have a clue. All he remembered was that he had said he might call that weekend, and he called and she hung up on him. A few weeks later he saw Rita at a meeting, and she'd cooled down enough to explain. Apparently she had thought they had a date for Saturday night—she was all ready and waiting, and he never called until Sunday night, when he acted like nothing was wrong.

Active Listening

Sorting it out, Vern came to realize that he had said something that sounded to Rita like he was asking her out on Saturday night. He thought he was just expressing an interest in seeing her again. When she accepted his request for a date, he thought she was just saying she enjoyed his company, too. Neither one of them had done anything to get clear on what the other was saying. They'd never learned active listening skills, which would have helped them avoid these kinds of misunderstandings. They thought about trying the date again, but neither of them felt particularly good about the other. They'd lost that basic sense of trust in one another.

> *Think about how many big problems in your life have been caused by little misunderstandings. It's much better to practice active listening skills than to make a disastrous mistake.*

Active listening skills are very simple. First you hear what the other person says. Then you say something like, "What I hear you saying is..." and you repeat word for word, or in your own words, what you believe the person has said. Then you ask, "Is that right?" Rita could have said, "What I hear you saying is that you really want to go to the fireworks on Saturday night, and you'd like to take me. Is that right?" She could have clarified it a little more by asking, "Are you asking me to go to the fireworks with you on Saturday night?"

Vern, who was thinking of several things at once and didn't really hear himself say that he'd like to take Rita to the fireworks, could have corrected it at that time. "I wish I could take you, but

I've already promised to go with my mother. It's something we do every year. I guess I got my thoughts jumbled up. What I really meant was that I like the fireworks, and I'd rather be going with you, because I really enjoy your company. I'd like to call you on Sunday and see if we can work something out for Sunday night." They could have made their own fireworks.

As simple as the skills of active listening are, they can be the hardest things in the world to remember to do. It's the most normal human tendency in the world to be sure that what we think we hear people saying is exactly what they mean. It feels silly to say, "What I hear you saying is.... Have I got that right?" with each statement they make. But think about how many big problems in your life have been caused by little misunderstandings. And ask people who know these skills what happens when they forget to use them. Considering how much we need to be able to trust and be trusted, it's much better to practice these skills until we sound silly than it would be to make a disastrous mistake.

Thought and Discussion Questions

1. When was the last time you failed to clarify something someone said, and later regretted it?
2. What might you have said to clarify it?
3. What steps might you take to learn and practice active listening skills?
4. What steps might you take to remind yourself to use these skills?

Building a Sober Social Network

Before sobriety, many people learned to focus on having a partner and to think of other friends and acquaintances as much less important. Before her divorce and entry into treatment, Ellen had only the friends she and Frank had made as a couple. When her sponsor asked her to make a list of the people in her support network, she had to admit that she had no network.

> **Sober social networks:**
> - Provide safe places to meet people
> - Help you develop new social values
> - Help you find the winners

Safety in Early Recovery

At its best, early recovery is like a safe, sober adolescence—the kind that many recovering people never had. You can make friends and get to know people without the pressure of expecting to get sexually involved. You can watch people from a safe distance and keep an eye out for high-risk people.

When you were out there drinking and drugging, the steps toward finding a partner probably went something like this: You go to the party, or the bar, or the street corner. You meet somebody. You ask them out, or they ask you out. You go out, and you get sexually involved. That was usually the game—whether or not you were successful at it. Many people in early recovery are still trying to play the same game, substituting the word "meeting" for "bar." It often causes problems and sometimes leads to relapse.

> *Many people in early recovery are still trying to play the same sexual conquest games they used to play, substituting the word "meeting" for "bar." It causes problems and sometimes leads to relapse.*

New Values in Early Recovery

In recovery, a person's well-being matters more than sex, more than words of love, more than diamond engagement rings. Your security is no longer tied up in sexual conquests or commitment. It's tied up in your willingness to grow and change, to open up and be honest, to care about the sobriety of both people—to care so much that you back off if one of you isn't ready to get involved safely. That's a radical change. To make that change effectively,

148

you need to get to know people—beyond the faces they wear, beyond the comments they make at meetings—before you even decide whether or not you want to get involved.

Sober Social Networks

Where can you get to know people safely? In sober social networks. These are the people you call once in a while, go out with for coffee or dinner after meetings, or run into at sober dances and parties. But not all people you meet in meetings are safe or healthy to hang around with. There are plenty of people who use meetings as hunting grounds for sexual or romantic victims. There are people whose life is just one drama after another, and you're valuable only as an audience. And there are people who are on their way to relapse and wouldn't mind taking you with them.

> *In recovery, people's well-being matters more than sex, more than words of love, more than diamond engagement rings. Your security is no longer tied up in sexual conquests or commitment.*

Finding the Winners

You've probably heard people say, "Stick with the winners." Just who are these winners, anyway? Are they the people who have many years' recovery? Are they the cool people, who act confident and wear the latest clothes? Are they the ones who have been financially successful in sobriety? But what about all the people who have lots of clean time and are still going around trying to control people? What about the people who are cool on the outside and falling apart on the inside? What about all the financially successful people who can't find the time for their recovery program?

To find the winners, you have to follow your "gut" instincts. After a few failed friendships in AA, Tammy stopped trying to find people who looked like winners, and started paying attention to the way she felt around them. She noticed that some people's comments at meetings made a lot of sense and helped her in the days that followed. They appeared to be happy and peaceful in their own lives. She wanted to be more like them. And when she talked to them, she felt good about herself. She felt like she didn't have to do anything special to be accepted by them, except be herself—as much or as little of herself as she understood at the time.

These were the people Tammy started asking for phone numbers, going out to coffee with, and calling once in a while. Some of these people became lasting friends and introduced her to other friends. Before long she had a social network that made it impossible for her to feel lonely. She often met new people. If she met an attractive man who seemed much like the men who had been bad for her before, she could pass him by. She knew she'd be meeting other men as time went by. She didn't need to jump at one possibility simply because she didn't know of any others at the moment.

Thought and Discussion Questions

1. Think of a recovering person you know whom you'd like to have as part of your social network. What's the most important thing you've learned from this person's comments?
2. What draws you to this person?
3. What qualities does this person have that you'd like to have?
4. How do you feel about yourself when you're with this person?

The Five Levels of Relationships

Sober social networks also allow you to let relationships develop slowly and naturally, coming to know and trust people a little bit at a time. Healthy romantic relationships tend to pass through five levels:

1. **Acquaintanceship:** You meet casually, with no real commitment.

2. **Companionship:** You get together for the purpose of sharing activities.

3. **Friendship:** You get together to get to know one another and spend time together.

4. **Romantic Love:** You're true friends and sexual partners.

5. **Committed Love:** You share life responsibilities and make commitments to meet one another's needs.

These levels build, one upon the others. Many people move quickly to romantic or sexual involvement without taking the time first to be companions, then friends. They think what they have is romantic love, but it's really a superficial acquaintanceship without the formality of clothing. Let's look at what can happen when people take it slowly, level by level.

Cal and Ruth didn't really notice one another at first. They lived on different social levels and had different styles of dressing and relating to the world. Cal was the artsy type, and Ruth was a corporate vice president. But they often wound up at the same end of the restaurant table after the Friday night meeting, and they appreciated one another's sense of humor. They spent a long time on the first level of relationship, as acquaintances.

One night Cal's car was in the shop and Ruth gave him a ride home after dinner. They discovered that they lived two blocks apart, so they started driving to meetings together and feeding one another's cats when one of them went out of town. Once in a while they'd get together to rent a video that they both wanted to watch. They finally had to give up the stereotyped notions they'd formed about one another from the beginning. In this phase they were on the companionship level. They were both careful about giving one another personal information, testing bit by bit to see how far they could trust one another.

> **Sober social networks give you a chance to grow slowly and safely through the five levels of relationship:**
> 1. Acquaintanceship
> 2. Companionship
> 3. Friendship
> 4. Romantic Love
> 5. Committed Love

Over time, Cal and Ruth started learning more and more about one another's lives, and they came to care about one another. Sometimes they'd drop over just to talk, and when one of them went through a hard time, the other was there for comfort and support. These two people who once thought they had nothing in common had become true friends.

Well, you guessed it: One day Cal realized that he was attracted to Ruth, and he asked her out on a date. She was a little suspicious, but when she thought about it, she realized she was attracted to him. After a few dates they moved into romantic and sexual involvement. Because they'd been getting to know each other over such a long period of time, they found that they loved one another deeply, and their desire was quite intense.

> **Good reasons for going slowly in relationships:**
> - Weed out the crazy people and high-risk partners
> - Let trust develop slowly over time
> - Build true intimacy
> - It will protect you through the growth and changes of sobriety
> - By focusing on your recovery, you'll become a better person to the relationship

In their characteristic slow fashion, Cal and Ruth took a few more years before they decided to get engaged, and their engagement lasted two years. On the level of committed love, it's become clear that their relationship is rock-solid, and their deep friendship has weathered many years' worth of challenges.

Thought and Discussion Questions

1. Have you been in any relationships that moved slowly over the levels described above? If so, how would you describe those relationships?
2. Have you been in any relationships that moved quickly over those levels, or skipped one or more levels to get to romantic or committed status? If so, how would you describe those relationships?
3. Which kind of relationship tended to bring you more pain and trouble: the one described in your answer to question 1, or your answer to question 2? Please explain.
4. What steps might you take to try to move slowly and consciously over those levels in your current or future relationships?

For most people in our culture—and especially for people with a history of addictive behavior—the idea of moving slowly through relationships might seem anywhere from unnecessary to excruciatingly painful. But it has several purposes. First, you can weed out the crazy people and your high-risk partners before you get close enough to get hurt. Second, you can develop trust slowly over time. This will allow you to build true intimacy, instead of forcing sex into a superficial relationship. And it will protect you through some of the slow and painful growth and changes that you have to go through during early recovery. When you do get involved, you'll contribute to the relationship as a happier, healthier human being.

Chapter 8

Middle Recovery

After almost four years' sobriety, Zena was getting impatient. She was ready for a relationship—way past ready, if you asked her. It wasn't as though she'd been fighting them off, either. She'd gone out with five or six men in recovery, but the longest those relationships had lasted was a month or so. The men always turned out to be crazy, or boring, or just not compatible with her. Whenever she asked her sponsor what was wrong, she got something like, "How's your eighth-step list coming along?" (The eighth-step list is a list of all people you've harmed.) Zena finally finished the list just to shut her up, and started contacting people to make amends for the mistakes she'd made in the past.

In this chapter, you'll look at:

- Relationship recovery tasks in middle recovery
- Being single in middle recovery
- Relationships in middle recovery

A lot of those people were former boyfriends, from her years of drinking. She also had an ex-husband and two ex-stepchildren whom she hadn't seen in nearly eight years. These amends scared her a little bit, but she was committed to her recovery. She also knew by now that difficult tasks grew more difficult the longer she put them off.

A few months later she was sitting at a kitchen table with Megan, one of her former stepdaughters, now a young woman at the age of twenty-one. Megan was a little shy, but trying to make Zena feel better as they sat there making conversation and watching the rain roll down the kitchen windows. "We didn't really understand," Megan said, "but Dad told us you had a problem and you had to run away." The tears started up in Zena's eyes as she realized why she'd never been able to hold down a relationship. All her life, all she'd ever done was run away. Now she had to learn how to stand her ground, and she didn't know how to do it.

Relationship Recovery Tasks in Middle Recovery

If early recovery is the opportunity for a safe adolescence, middle recovery is an opportunity to be an adult. This stage is all about responsibility. Its overall goal is lifestyle balance. It includes repairing the damage you did in your years of drinking and drugging, and building a balanced life where you do things that will keep your body and mind healthy. The eighth and ninth steps (a list of people harmed and an attempt to repair that damage) are important in this stage, because they give you a structure in which you can "make amends"—mend your relationships with people—and make a connection with the world.

Relationship recovery tasks of middle recovery:
- Developing balanced, healthy relationships that fit your new lifestyle
- Attracting sober or nonaddicted partners
- Losing your addiction to the "using" lifestyle

In middle recovery the primary focus is developing a healthy lifestyle balance to support sobriety and responsibility. Recovery tasks in this stage include working on solutions to the problems in your life; setting up a program of physical health and balance; learning to manage your thoughts, feelings, urges, and actions more effectively; and learning to act and communicate in healthy ways in all your relationships. If you're in a long-term relationship, this stage may be the strongest test of that relationship so far. If you're not in a relationship, this stage may be the first time it's really safe to start one.

As you develop a sober lifestyle, you'll need to integrate your relationships into that lifestyle. It's important to be involved only with people who are clean and sober, or nonaddicted. Often chemically dependent people aren't just addicted to the drug; they're addicted to the lifestyle. In sobriety, if you want your relationships to fit in with your new lifestyle, you'll need to cultivate relationships with emotionally healthy people who don't abuse alcohol or drugs.

> *Before you're ready to offer yourself as a romantic partner—or even know what kind of partner would be good for you—you need to look at who you are right now.*

Being Single in Middle Recovery

If you're still single in middle recovery, you might be starting to be glad you are. After the addictive thinking has calmed down a little bit, and you're able to see yourself and your life more clearly, you might be surprised at how much you still need to change. You'll never have a perfect life to share with a partner, but you can clean up some of the messes before you invite someone in. The sixth, seventh, eighth, and ninth steps are excellent tools (becoming willing to give up self-defeating behaviors, accepting help in that process, listing the people you've harmed, and making amends). So is therapy, and so are relationship recovery groups. The desire for a relationship can be an excellent excuse

157

to take care of the problems we really need to take care of for our own sake.

What You Have to Offer as a Partner

Before you're ready to offer yourself as a romantic partner— or even know what kind of partner would be good for you—you need to look at who you are right now. Spending time with your sober social network has probably given you a lot of important information about yourself. Your sixth through ninth steps can give you even more information. Answer the questions below as they're true today, rather than as they were when you were out there drinking and drugging. Answer them as if no one will ever see what you've written, but as if the success of your relationships will depend on your honesty.

Thought and Discussion Questions

1. What's the best quality you have to offer a partner, and why is it valuable in a relationship?
2. What are some other qualities you like in yourself and/ or qualities that others appreciate in you?
3. What defects in your personality tend to cause the most problems in relationships?
4. What are some other defects in your personality that have caused problems in your relationships?
5. How do you express or repress (hold in) anger in your relationships?
6. How do you deal with conflict in your relationships? (What do you do in times of conflict?)
7. What are two ways that you put some distance between you and other people to keep relationships from getting too close?
8. What are two ways you can stop doing those things that create distance?

---

9. What is the difference between closeness and intimacy?
10. What are two ways you tend to hurt your relationships without being aware that you're doing it?
11. What are two steps you can take to change these behaviors?

Knowing what you have to contribute to a relationship is an important part of attracting the right relationship. Knowing what you need to change—and taking steps to change it—is an important part of staying away from the wrong relationships and not ruining the right ones.

Single by Choice

What if you wonder whether or not you want to be in a relationship at all? Jerry thought maybe something was wrong with him because he didn't want a romantic or committed relationship. The women he had dated told him he was afraid to love. He tried to be the partner they wanted, but he couldn't. He liked to have sex once in a while, but he didn't want anything deeper. Finally a former girlfriend suggested that he just tell women how he felt, honestly and openly, before he began to get involved. That way no one would get false expectations, and no one would feel the weight of those expectations.

Some people simply aren't romantic, and some people simply aren't monogamous by nature. Some people aren't particularly sexual. Whether it's fear that makes them that way or just something different in their nature, it doesn't matter. We are whoever we are at this moment, no matter how we got this way or how we'll change in the future. Not wanting a relationship is not a problem. The only problem would be pretending to want a relationship—or thinking you were supposed to want one—when you didn't.

So if all this talk about relationships is foreign and confusing to you, don't worry about it. Truly intimate relationships can be very rewarding, but they can also be very difficult and painful. If you're single by choice, that's a perfectly honorable way to be, as long as you're honest about it. That choice might change in the future, or it might not. What matters is that you're true to yourself as you are now.

Recognizing Appropriate Partners

If you've spent most of your dating life with your high-risk partners, you might feel a bit frustrated when it comes to partner selection. You might be a Geiger counter for men or women who are attractive but destructive to you. You may even have learned that the people who attract you most quickly and most strongly are the ones you should stay away from.

Raquel was convinced that no man could love her because every man she'd been in love with had been unable to return her feelings. They liked her and wanted her sexually, but she just wasn't the type they fell for. She was very independent, and the men she was involved with always seemed to fall for helpless, needy women. She assumed that all men were like that, and felt that her independence made her somehow defective.

Then one day a man in her singles recovery group told her, "I can't stand helpless, needy women. I never fall for helpless women, and neither do any of my friends. Maybe there's a whole bunch of us out here who want independent women, but your radar is only set up to lock onto the other kind." So she started thinking about the qualities of her former boyfriends that made them want or need helpless women. They were usually somewhat self-centered and closed off emotionally. She never needed anything from them, and they never gave anything. Then when they met someone who really needed them, it broke through their armor and they were finally able to give of themselves.

So Raquel started looking around at the men who were the opposite of her high-risk partners. These were the men who were open and giving, and wore their emotions close to the skin. She realized she was a little uncomfortable around these men and tended not to notice them or to think about them as prospective partners. She wondered about that, and wondered how many other "types" of men she wasn't noticing. She decided not to give up on relationships until she'd taken a little more time to understand what her options were and what she really wanted or needed in a partner.

Thought and Discussion Questions

1. What are three of the most important qualities you look for in a friend?
2. Have these qualities also been present in your romantic partners? Please explain.
3. Describe what your parents taught you—directly or indirectly—about choosing a partner.
4. What is your greatest fear about future relationships?
5. What are two steps you can take toward overcoming this fear without using?
6. What types of people tend to make you feel good about yourself?
7. What types of people tend to make you feel bad about yourself?
8. What is the most important way a partner can support your recovery?
9. If you take good care of your own physical, mental, emotional, and spiritual needs, how will that affect your relationship?
10. What steps can you take to avoid partners who are unhealthy for you?

If the person who would be best for you is not the person you tend to attract or be attracted to, don't worry. That's normal at this stage of recovery. You don't have to get sexually involved with people you don't desire, or swear off the ones you do desire. But it will be helpful if you just try to expand your vision a little more, so that you start to notice all kinds of people. Little by little your world will grow larger, and your sense of possibility will grow stronger. You don't yet know all there is to know about who you are and what you truly want in your life. You're not supposed to know. You have time to learn.

> *Not wanting a relationship is not a problem. The only problem would be pretending to want a relationship—or thinking you were supposed to want one—when you didn't.*

Healthy Relationships in Middle Recovery

In this strange, adult world that is middle recovery, we need to learn a whole new sense of responsibility where relationships are concerned. This includes getting a clear sense of where our responsibilities begin and end, being present and authentic in our relationships, and basing our relationships on our deepest values.

Cleaning Up Your Side of the Street

You've probably heard people in the program talk about "keeping your side of the street clean." But even finding your side of the street, and keeping it separate from the other person's side, is hard. Most of us have been taught since earliest childhood to take responsibility for other people's feelings and actions, and/or give them responsibility for ours. How many recovering people, in completing their eighth-step lists (of people harmed), were tempted to cross off the people who had also hurt them? It's hard to make amends to someone who owes amends to you. But in middle recovery, the time has come to let go of other people's mistakes and simply take responsibility for your own.

Regaining Dignity

Dick's ex-wife was still "The Ex from Hell" when he approached her on his ninth step (an attempt to "make amends" and repair the damage done in the past). He knew she would see it as an opportunity to rip into some of his more vulnerable spots, and she did. But he stood there and said what he had to say in a calm voice. As he said it he realized that he really had hurt her and the kids. He hadn't caused her to react the way she did—that was her choice—but he did owe her amends. As he walked away, he realized two things: He was no longer afraid of her, and he had his dignity back.

Building healthy relationships in middle recovery includes:
- Cleaning up your side of the street
- Regaining your dignity
- Finding your boundaries
- Being present and authentic
- Building relationships around values

Finding Boundaries

People in recovery talk a lot about boundaries; it's a very useful concept. A boundary is the dividing line between your responsibilities and someone else's. Knowing what the boundaries were made it possible for Dick to honestly regret the way he had neglected his wife and children when he was active in his addiction. This was true even though her actions had been less than charitable at the time, and he used to blame her for everything that went wrong. He knew that he now had great hope of success in his future relationships. Now that he had learned the difference between his side of the street and someone else's, he intended never to forget it again.

> *A boundary is the dividing line between your responsibilities and someone else's.*

It's no coincidence that many people recovering in AA, NA, and CA tend to try out meetings of Al-Anon, ACOA, Coc-Anon, and the like in the middle recovery years. Those programs are designed to help people focus on their own "stuff," even when it's most tempting to focus on someone else's. That clearly defined focus is one of the great secrets of a healthy relationship. Without it, we can't take care of ourselves or respect our partners.

Thought and Discussion Questions

1. Describe one instance when you felt responsible for someone else's reaction to something you did or said.
2. Describe one instance when you felt that someone else "made" you feel a certain way, do what you did, or say what you said.
3. What are three consequences you fear might happen as a result of your setting a boundary in your relationship?
4. What are some steps you might take to keep your responsibilities separate from those of other people?

Being Present and Authentic

One of the great benefits of alcohol and other drugs was the hiding place they provided. You didn't have to be yourself, or be honest about what you thought or felt. You could "check out" any time things got too tense or too unfamiliar. In sobriety, you may have noticed that there are still many hiding places in relationships. People-pleasing is one of them. Manipulation is another. Guilt works very well, and so does rage. All of these kinds of states protect us from our vulnerability as human beings with needs, wants, feelings, and opinions.

Sylvia never understood why her boyfriend kept losing patience with her. She tried to please him every way she could. What she wasn't willing to do was tell him she believed he was wrong when he believed he was right, or to tell him what she needed from him when he was giving what he thought he should give. She didn't want to be demanding, and she didn't want to drive him away. She finally enrolled in an assertiveness training course, where she learned that being assertive is different from being loud, demanding, and obnoxious.

> *One of the "benefits" of alcohol and drugs was the hiding place they provided. You didn't have to be yourself or be honest. In sobriety, there are still many hiding places in relationships.*

After she had worked on an assertiveness style that fit her personality, Sylvia found she was still having trouble stating her wants and needs. In couples therapy, she discovered that she simply didn't trust him enough to be honest with him, whatever being honest meant at any given moment. She had never really trusted any partner. They made a commitment to work on it together.

Thought and Discussion Questions

1. How do you express or repress distrust in relationships?
2. How do you express or repress fear of commitment in relationships?
3. How do you feel before you express your feelings in an important relationship?
4. How do you feel after you express your feelings in an important relationship?
5. What's the most difficult thing for you about expressing feelings in a relationship?

Building Relationships Around Values

It doesn't seem fair that human beings are so often attracted to one another based on superficial things, when it's our deepest values that determine lifelong compatibility. Jeff had been in recovery four years, and he and Karla had been in couples counseling together for a year. They were both confused about why their relationship wasn't working better. They'd reached an uneasy truce that held most of the time, but each time the conflict flared up, the bitterness grew worse.

Finally they had to admit they'd just grown apart. Their values had never been very similar, but that fact was lost in the conflict that his drinking caused, and the turbulence of early recovery. The more involved he became in his program, the less they had in common. He became less concerned with achievement and material success, and happier in a lower-paid helping profession. She still wanted the old lifestyle they had had before his chemical dependency forced him to look at his priorities. They finally broke up, sad but more than a little relieved.

> *It doesn't seem fair that human beings are so often attracted to one another based on superficial things, when it's our deepest values that determine lifelong compatibility.*

Drew and Margie's situation also looked bleak for a while, but in counseling they discovered that they really did believe in and care deeply about the same things in life. Maybe they'd known that in the beginning, but it had been lost under all the conflict. Their task now was to work on the skills of honesty, openness, and mutual support that would help them uncover the true basis of their relationship. It wasn't easy, but it worked.

The following pairs of values are ones that don't necessarily conflict, but we sometimes have to choose between them, just because of the way life goes.

Values Chart

For each line of paired values, put an "X" on the line next to the one you'd be most likely to choose if you had to. If you really don't know, put the X in the space between the lines. *Hint*: If you're having trouble deciding which value you would choose, look at which values you've tended to choose in your sobriety. Our actions speak louder than our intentions.

Freedom	_____	_____	Commitment
Having nice things	_____	_____	Saving money
Fun	_____	_____	Achievement
Excitement	_____	_____	Stability
Humor	_____	_____	Depth
Forgiveness	_____	_____	Justice
Life experience	_____	_____	Education
Inspiration	_____	_____	Hard work
Change	_____	_____	Loyalty
Financial status	_____	_____	Service to others

Unfortunately, sometimes even the strongest love and the clearest, most compatible boundaries and values aren't enough to keep people from hurting one another. Unhealed wounds from childhood can cause each partner to "push the other's buttons" in ways that are painful to both partners. The next chapter discusses late recovery, the stage in which many of the wounds from childhood are discovered and healed.

Relationship Profile Assessment

For each of the four categories below, check all the words that apply.

When I'm involved in a healthy relationship, I tend to be:

☐ Responsive	☐ Humorous	☐ Giving	☐ Playful
☐ Receptive	☐ Sensual	☐ Respectful	☐ Secure
☐ Affectionate	☐ Forgiving	☐ Thoughtful	☐ Open-minded
☐ Trusting	☐ Sexual	☐ Sensitive	☐ Honest
☐ Good-natured	☐ Flexible	☐ Sharing	☐ Interdependent
	☐ Adventurous	☐ Caring	☐ Assertive

Which of these words best describes you in a healthy relationship?_____

When I'm involved in a healthy relationship, I tend to pick partners who are:

☐ Responsive	☐ Humorous	☐ Giving	☐ Playful
☐ Receptive	☐ Sensual	☐ Respectful	☐ Secure
☐ Affectionate	☐ Forgiving	☐ Thoughtful	☐ Open-minded
☐ Trusting	☐ Sexual	☐ Sensitive	☐ Honest
☐ Good-natured	☐ Flexible	☐ Sharing	☐ Interdependent
	☐ Adventurous	☐ Caring	☐ Assertive

Which of these words best describes your partner in a healthy relationship?

_____

When I'm involved in an addictive relationship, I tend to be:

☐ Jealous	☐ Clinging	☐ Guarded	☐ Aggressive
☐ Domineering	☐ Suspicious	☐ Secretive	☐ Manipulative
☐ Remote	☐ Avoiding	☐ Unaffectionate	☐ Inappropriate
☐ Obsessive	☐ Judgmental	☐ Passive	☐ Fearful
☐ Rigid	☐ Punitive	☐ Unforgiving	☐ Closed Minded
☐ Rejecting	☐ Self-centered	☐ Other-centered	☐ Dependent

Which of these words best describes you in an addictive relationship?_____

When I'm involved in an addictive relationship, I tend to pick partners who are:

☐ Jealous	☐ Clinging	☐ Guarded	☐ Aggressive
☐ Domineering	☐ Suspicious	☐ Secretive	☐ Manipulative
☐ Remote	☐ Avoiding	☐ Unaffectionate	☐ Inappropriate
☐ Obsessive	☐ Judgmental	☐ Passive	☐ Fearful
☐ Rigid	☐ Punitive	☐ Unforgiving	☐ Closed Minded
☐ Rejecting	☐ Self-centered	☐ Other-centered	☐ Dependent

Which of these words best describes your partner in an addictive relationship?_____

Chapter 9

Late Recovery

Darrin and LaDonna seemed like the perfect couple. Each one worked a solid recovery program, and they were both well respected by their friends. They were great together, and people truly enjoyed being with them. But whenever they spent more than three days in a row together, they started to have serious problems. A lot of little things Darrin did would bother LaDonna quite a bit. She'd try to keep her concerns to herself, because if she did point these problems out, Darrin would start pulling away from her and doing even more things that bothered her. The more hurt she felt, the more she tried to ask him for help. The more she did that, the farther away he seemed to draw. They would always end up with deeply hurt feelings, serious fighting, and a fear of being honest with one another about how they felt.

In this chapter, you'll look at:
- The challenges of late recovery
- The effects of childhood wounds on relationships
- Successful relationships in Late Recovery

They knew that each one had experienced a lot of pain in childhood; in many ways this pain felt the same. But they'd both been through therapy, and they understood their childhood histories thoroughly. They thought they were done with all that. But it soon became clear that each one was triggering some of the old thoughts, feelings, and actions that the other one had used to get through a troubled childhood.

The Challenges of Late Recovery

After they've done good work on the tasks of middle recovery, many people find a troubling surprise waiting for them: Childhood problems that they thought they'd understood and resolved are still coming out—sometimes intensely—in their relationships. We call this the late recovery stage. Not everyone has to go through this stage, because not everyone grew up in a family or community that was troubled by addiction or other dysfunction. Not everyone had to spend time in a home, neighborhood, school, church, or other institution that felt dangerous to them. Not everyone experienced intense pain and fear with no appropriate way to work through the pain and fear.

> *The main task of relationship recovery in late recovery is to use those relationships as a source of healing, rather than just a trigger for addictive behavior.*

The tasks of late recovery include recognizing childhood issues, getting accurate information about your family of origin, mapping out your childhood history as you remember it, understanding the connection between your childhood coping styles and your problems as an adult, and changing your adult lifestyle to reflect the healing of childhood wounds.

Relationship Recovery Tasks in Late Recovery

Romantic relationships are excellent helpers in the process of recovery from childhood experiences. More than any other kind of situation, these relationships tend to bring any unhealed childhood "stuff" to the surface. We're often drawn into love relationships with partners who have both the good and bad qualities of our primary caregivers. These similarities tend to be powerful triggers both for sexual attraction and for the feeling of being in love with someone. So when you get into relationships in late recovery, you often fall back into self-defeating patterns and start acting in ways your parents used to act when you were a child.

The main task of relationship recovery in late recovery is to use those relationships as a source of healing, rather than just a trigger for addictive behavior. Understanding what's happening is the first step. Getting help is the next. It's important to understand that your partner isn't your enemy. It's also important to understand that your intense attraction may not be a sign that you truly love your partner and belong with him or her. It might just be a sign that something in you needs to be healed.

Problems in Late Recovery

If you're in a relationship in late recovery, you've probably been experiencing problems that "shouldn't be happening" with all the recovery you've achieved. If you're not in a relationship, you'll probably recognize these problems as the ones that have destroyed former relationships, or kept you from taking the risk of getting so close to another human being. The work of late recovery is hard work, and is sometimes painful. But it's less painful than what happens if you don't do this work, and it's necessary for your own peace of mind and the success of your relationships.

Resolving Problems on Deeper Levels

What about all the good, hard work you did on your fourth step (personal inventory) and the time you spent in therapy in the early years of sobriety? What about the forgiveness you may have accomplished in order to complete your ninth step (making amends)? Why weren't these issues put to rest during your years of looking at your childhood clearly and honestly? Your hard work was valuable, but as the years progress, these problems often need to be understood and resolved on deeper and deeper levels of your being. No matter how smart you were or how hard you worked on yourself earlier, it probably wasn't safe for you to experience these issues at the depth that you're experiencing them now.

If you had trauma as a child—intense fear that was not dealt with effectively at the time—you may well be suffering from post-traumatic stress disorder (PTSD), the condition described more fully on pages 115–116. You might just now be remembering things that happened to you when you were a child. There may be experiences you'll never remember, and that's as it should be. At any stage of recovery, if a memory is **repressed** (hidden from your conscious awareness), that means it would neither be safe nor helpful to remember it at this time. Contrary to what psychologists used to believe, you can heal the effects of a situation without remembering it thoroughly.

As the years progress, the problems instilled in childhood often need to be understood and resolved on deeper and deeper levels of your being.

Don't go poking around in your mind trying to find or reconstruct memories, even with the help of a therapist. You'll remember when it's time to remember. The subconscious mind has an amazing wisdom of its own. We don't need to interfere with its work. Our only responsibility is to get appropriate professional help when painful memories start to surface.

Thought and Discussion Questions

1. Have you been experiencing any problems in your life and relationships that don't seem to make sense given the amount of time and effort you've put into your recovery? Please explain.
2. Read the description of PTSD on page 51. Have you ever experienced any of those symptoms? Please describe them.
3. If you've had lost childhood memories return to you in sobriety, what steps have you taken to get help in coping with those memories?
4. What other steps might you take for your own safety and sobriety?

174

Issues of Loyalty and Forgiveness

Many people who are thoroughly committed to full recovery still find it hard to look honestly at the mistakes that parents and other family members may have made. It might be part of their culture, or their family culture, not to question parents and others in authority. Their parents might have been deeply wounded in their own childhood and did the best they could to raise their children. The family might have been plagued by bad luck or surrounded by unfriendly people or dangerous circumstances. Saying or thinking negative things about family members might feel like a betrayal.

Ricardo's alcoholic father loved his family deeply. As vividly as Ricardo remembered his father's rage and his blows, he also remembered the scars his father had carried from his own childhood, and the courage and honor with which he cared for his family through years of poverty. All the rules of his culture told him he had no right to talk about his father in couples therapy sessions.

For some people, it's harder to address childhood wounds because saying or thinking negative things about family members feels like a betrayal.

Finally his fiancée asked him, "What about your loyalty to me? What about your loyalty to the children we're going to have? If you keep treating me this way, how are you going to treat our children? You may never hit us, but you'll never be able to see us as free human beings. Unless you talk about this stuff here, you're just going to pass it on to them."

Anger at a family member who hurt you can also feel like a betrayal of family loyalty. Forgiveness is an important part of healing. It's a letting go of the wrongs others have done, whether or not those wrongs were excusable. It frees us from the burdens of the past. But sometimes forgiveness hides a denial of the anger that's still inside. If we forgive too quickly, without feeling our anger thoroughly, have we really forgiven?

175

Often anger and forgiveness come in layers. It's common for people in late recovery to feel intense anger over injuries they thought they had forgiven completely in early recovery. Katy was surprised to learn how angry she was in therapy at the memories she had of her mother. The forgiveness she had achieved in early recovery was real, and it was necessary to free her mind for the tasks of early recovery. But the anger was real, too, and she would have to deal with it if she ever wanted to have a successful relationship.

Thought and Discussion Questions

1. Do you in any way feel you're being disloyal if you speak in negative terms about people in your family or events in your childhood?
2. Who might you be betraying if you fail to heal the wounds from your childhood? Please explain your answer.
3. How hard or easy is it for you to forgive people whose actions might have hurt you in your childhood?
4. How might it be possible to be loyal to someone, and learn to forgive that person, but still feel anger for a while?

The Effects of Childhood Wounds on Relationships

It would take a long book—several long books—to cover all the effects a troubled family or traumatic event can have on a child and what these effects can do to relationships. This section will give you a short introduction, including a little information on what children learn in families, the coping skills children develop, the role of childhood experiences in determining who seems attractive in adulthood, and the role of intimacy in bringing out the issues that need to be healed.

What Children Learn in Families

When you think about what you learned in your family as a child, don't just think about the things your parents and other authority figures told you about life and about what you should do. Think more about what they did, the example you automatically learned to follow—because that's what children do. Think about the messages hidden underneath what your family members said. You had no choice but to believe these messages. You had no choice but to follow as many of their examples as it was safe to follow and to make up other ways of coping.

What Healthy Families Teach

Healthy or functional families teach children that it's safe to look honestly at themselves and the world around them. They learn that they're basically OK and they don't have to pretend they're something they're not. They learn to honestly experience and talk about what's happening around them. They don't have to pretend that problems don't exist or that things are worse than they really are.

In functional families children learn that both thinking and feeling are good, and they learn to balance those functions and use them appropriately. They learn to think clearly, logically, and rationally. They also learn to identify, describe, and communicate their true feelings. They learn that both pleasant and unpleasant feelings are OK to have. They don't have to pretend to feel good when they don't, or try to escape their unpleasant feelings.

What Troubled Families Teach

In most troubled families, children learn ways of thinking that lead to confusion and inner conflict. They learn to believe in ideas that have no basis in reality. Roy's father taught him that he must be strong, no matter what. As a child, Roy learned that he must never cry or talk about his problems. Whenever he felt the fear and sadness that are a normal part of being human, Roy was thrown into conflict and self-hatred.

> **Healthy families teach children:**
>
> - It's safe to look honestly at themselves and the world.
> - They're basically OK.
> - They don't have to pretend they're something they're not.
> - They can talk honestly about what's happening to them and around them.
> - Both thinking and feeling are good.
>
> **Unhealthy families teach children:**
>
> - It's better to stay confused.
> - They're basically worthless or not good enough.
> - They can't talk honestly about what's happening.
> - Their thoughts and feelings can't be trusted.

Children often learn that it's better to stay confused, because what you see and what your family is telling you may be two very different things. Painful feelings are also thought of as bad, and children learn to block out the awareness of pain or try to escape that pain in any way possible. Children learn that who they are is basically worthless or not good enough. They learn to give up on themselves or try too hard to win the approval they can never quite get.

The Effects of Families of Origin on Relationships

You can imagine the impact of these lessons on relationships. It's hard to have a healthy relationship when you've learned to keep your thoughts confused and to deny or escape unpleasant feelings. If you learned as a child that you weren't good enough, you're likely to feel all of your partner's negative moods or comments as evidence that you're not good enough. You may try to find all of your self-worth in your partner's love for you, a burden that no love can carry.

The beliefs that we learn as children can cause problems in adult relationships, too. When Roy's mother died, he couldn't allow himself to feel his grief, and he shut his girlfriend out of his life completely. Her presence reminded him of his love, and so it reminded him of his pain and his vulnerability—two things he was not allowed to have.

Conflicting Beliefs

Often in relationships, two partners are operating under two very different sets of beliefs. Each one, by doing what he or she was always taught to do, often violates the other one's rules. June's family taught her that no one was ever supposed to say anything critical, no matter what they were thinking. Whenever her boyfriend had a negative reaction to something she had said or done, it felt as if he was deliberately hurting her. She couldn't believe he would act that way. But in his family when he was growing up, that was the way he was supposed to act.

Thought and Discussion Questions

1. When you were a child, how did your primary caregiver show approval?
2. How did your primary caregiver show disapproval?
3. How did your primary caregiver show love or affection?
4. How do you think your primary caregiver's ways of expressing these things have affected the way you feel about yourself?
5. How do you think your primary caregiver's influence has affected your relationships?
6. How did your primary caregiver tell you or not tell you about love, commitment, and marriage?
7. What did your primary caregiver tell you or not tell you about sex and sexuality?

The beliefs that you learned in your family might also have played a role in shaping your answers to the core questions of being single. Let's revisit those questions as you experience them today.

Children's Coping Skills

Many of the behaviors that are most troubling to your relationships—and may even be very annoying to you—might once have been necessary to help you survive and stay sane in your family of origin. They worked: you survived. In adult life, though, these same survival skills often cause problems. The circumstances have changed. Now in times of discomfort you're supposed to face the discomfort, work honestly through it, or just live with it for a while. But the automatic response is to go back to the survival skills that worked in childhood. Now these skills may be keeping you from being yourself, from being responsible, from being honest, or from being respectful to others.

Problems in Adult Life

Grace was always playing the clown, making a joke in every situation. This skill helped her take her family's attention away from the pain caused by her brother's chronic mental illness. It helped her cope with her social fears as an adolescent and from the problems caused by her drinking in later life. But even in late recovery, Grace found that her sense of humor still had a mind of its own. It would pop out in serious situations, sometimes making light of other people's fear and anger. It was driving her fiancé crazy.

> *Many of the behaviors that are most troubling to your relationships—and may even be very annoying to you—might once have been necessary to help you survive and stay sane in your family of origin.*

Earl's problem was his tendency to take care of people. That care had been necessary when he was a child and his mother entered the late stages of alcoholism. After he'd spent a while in recovery for his own addiction, he became a chemical dependency counselor and helped many people. But he was unable to sit back and let his girlfriend take care of the problems that she had to learn to take responsibility for solving. It was ruining his relationship and his peace of mind.

Stephanie was always feeling guilty and apologizing for her quick temper. But when she was a child, it was that temper that kept her from giving in to a constant stream of criticism and disapproval from the staff at the group home in which she was raised. She had used that temper to protect her dignity when her dignity was under attack, but in late recovery she still found it hard to relax and feel safe in any situation. Through the years her partners had felt hurt and insulted, and had given up on her in fairly short order.

Defects as Extremes of Assets

Often our most troublesome characteristics are extreme versions of qualities that are really strengths. Grace had a wonderful sense of humor. Earl was an excellent therapist. Stephanie had a lot of spunk and great debating skills. In late recovery each one had the task of learning—not to "get rid of" these qualities—but to tell when to exercise them and when to hold back. When Grace learned to hold her tongue in serious situations, people started taking her more seriously, and they were delighted when a really appropriate joke came out. Earl became a better therapist and a better partner when he learned to let people feel the effects of their mistakes. And Stephanie grew more courageous and effective when she learned to pick her battles. Their relationships improved dramatically.

Childhood Wounds and Attraction Patterns

Have you ever wondered why we're most often attracted to the people who end up pushing our buttons? It's because of a tendency called the "need to resolve." As you've seen, children learn to cope with the pain and trauma in their lives in whatever ways seem safe for them at the time. But as the years pass, the coping goes just so far.

Many people have a hidden need to resolve the hurt from childhood. Without being aware of it, they have a desire—born in childhood—to go through the same experience again and *make it come out differently*. Mick was almost always attracted to women who had chronic relapse problems and couldn't or wouldn't get help for those problems. In therapy he learned that he was still trying to get his mother sober. SueAnne was always attracted to men with strong tempers, even after she had enough recovery to know better. Something inside her wanted to relive her years of giving in to her older brother's temper, so she could come out the winner this time.

Unfortunately, when most people recreate their painful childhood experiences in adult relationships, they aren't able to make them turn out much better. There may be a few improvements: At least Mick's girlfriends were in AA and SueAnne's boyfriends didn't beat her up the way her brother did. But in those adult situations, most people keep on using the same coping skills they used to survive in childhood.

Making Situations Worse

Not only do those coping skills not fix the situations, they often make them worse. Mick would do anything to protect his partners from the effects of their actions, and so they were never forced to get the extra help they needed. SueAnne grew fearful and childlike when her boyfriends threw temper tantrums. Her reactions only increased their anger.

How do childhood experiences damage adult relationships?

- Partners are often operating from conflicting beliefs.
- The coping skills that helped in childhood now make things worse.
- Both partners may suffer from low self-esteem.
- Partners may be unconsciously trying to resolve childhood experiences by reliving them in adulthood.
- Intimacy triggers old ways of responding.

Identifying the Need to Resolve

In therapy and recovery work, you can learn to identify the ways your partner-attraction patterns might point to one or more members of your family of origin. Your attraction patterns won't automatically change, but your new awareness will help you look more honestly at your relationships. You can also learn to identify the coping skills that you use with your partners. You can learn and practice new skills that will make things better instead of worse. Ideally, you can get your partner's help in this process.

Thought and Discussion Questions

1. Think of your current partner, or your high-risk partner. Does this person treat you in any ways similar to the ways you were treated as a child? Please explain.
2. When this pattern arises, how do you react?
3. In what ways are these reactions similar to those you had as a child, and in what ways are they different?
4. What kinds of reactions might be more effective in your adult situations?

Intimacy as a Trigger

Why do romantic and sexual relationships bring out these problems so much more dramatically than other kinds of relationships? Our relationships in our families of origin were our earliest and strongest lessons about the meaning of closeness and intimacy. It makes sense that the closeness we often feel in adult intimate relationships would bring out any problems that we've "stored up" in this area.

> *Our relationships in our families of origin were our earliest and strongest lessons about the meaning of closeness and intimacy. The closeness in adult intimate relationships bring out any problems we've "stored up" in this area.*

In the case of Darrin and LaDonna described at the beginning of this chapter, they usually started to trigger one another only after they had spent more than a few days together. Over those few days, their feelings of closeness would grow and start to stir up the pain they usually managed to hide from themselves.

Many people find that closeness and true intimacy bring out strong fears of being trapped, or fears of being abandoned. To make things more difficult, people with strong fears of being trapped tend to be attracted to people who happen to have strong feelings of being abandoned. The reverse is also true: People with fears of being abandoned are attracted to people who fear being trapped. It's that old "need to resolve" working again. Someone who's afraid of being trapped is more likely to run away and abandon you. Someone who's afraid of being abandoned is more likely to cling to you. So you choose the partner who is most likely to do what you fear the most.

LaDonna's fear of abandonment came from her father's on-and-off relationship with her family when she was young. He and her mother were always fighting, and he walked out a dozen times while she was young, often staying away for several months. When Darrin didn't seem to be taking his responsibilities seriously enough, it would awaken her childhood fear of being left behind. She would hold her fears inside her until they came out in the form of demands and requests for emotional help. But Darrin's mother had looked to him for all the closeness and nurturing she needed when his father died. He had grown up with a strong fear of being trapped by a woman's needs and demands.

People who are afraid of being trapped tend to

- attract—and be attracted to—people who are afraid of being abandoned;
- do things that raise their partners' fears of abandonment; and
- inspire entrapping responses in their partners.

People who are afraid of being abandoned tend to

- attract—and be attracted to—people who are afraid of being trapped;
- do things that raise their partners' fears of being trapped; and
- inspire abandoning responses in their partners.

Healing the Fears

In couples therapy LaDonna finally realized that if she didn't do some serious work on her fear of abandonment, she really would drive him away. The fear itself would force the one thing she really didn't want to happen. And Darrin came to understand that when he drew away emotionally and closed her off from his affection, it only made her fear of abandonment grow worse. If he wanted some room to breathe, he would first have to learn to be there for her, needs and all. In other words, if they wanted their push-pull game to stop, she would have to stop pushing him, and he would have to stop pulling away.

Thought and Discussion Questions

1. In your relationships, have you experienced a fear of being trapped or a fear of being abandoned? Which fear has been stronger, and how have you known you had this fear?
2. Please describe any events or relationships in your childhood that might be connected to the fear of being trapped or abandoned?
3. When you feel a fear of being trapped or abandoned in a relationship, how do you react to your partner?
4. How have your reactions tended to hurt your relationships or keep them from growing?

Successful Relationships in Late Recovery

Many couples with serious family-of-origin problems have worked through those problems effectively and found peace and happiness together. Many others whose problems were much less serious have been driven apart by those problems. Some combinations of people just won't work no matter what you do. But more often, it's *both* partners' willingness to work on the relationship that determines success. If your partner isn't willing to work on it effectively, you won't be able to fix it alone. But if you're both willing to try to the best of your ability, you have a chance.

Learning to Communicate

Dale and Kim found it painful but, with the help of their relationship recovery group, they both learned to communicate honestly and openly about their strengths and their challenges in the relationship. They even learned to tell one another honestly—and without using dramatic or exaggerated terms—how they felt about each other's behavior and how it was affecting them.

> *If your partner isn't willing to work on it effectively, you won't be able to fix it alone. But if you're both willing to try to the best of your ability, you have a chance.*

Deciding What You Can and Can't Change

After a while it became clear that there were some ways each one was willing and able to change, and other ways they couldn't or wouldn't change. Dale was going to keep on being a police officer until retirement or death, even though it awakened a lot of old fears in Kim. Kim would never be the "tough cookie" that Dale had been raised to believe he needed in his life. They could talk honestly about those things, though, and they made their decision about whether or not to stay in the relationship based on what they could and couldn't accept.

The Danger of Overdoing It

If you're working through late-recovery problems with your partner, it's important to remember not to turn your relationship into an extended therapy session. Gena and Paul were doing such a good job of working on their issues that their therapist thought of them as her ideal client couple. One day in session Paul burst out with the news that he was going crazy talking about their stuff all the time. "I need some normal, adult time with you. We never get that. We spend way too much time talking about these problems and what we're doing to solve them. I need to just be together, to be quiet together, two people who love one another."

Once the immediate crisis is over, it's good to set some boundaries on your therapeutic conversations. You might want to save these conversations for sessions with your therapist, except when they're necessary to confront immediate problems or clear up misunderstandings. You might reserve a certain time of day to bring up any problems or issues to be discussed, or set a curfew for these kinds of discussions. You can work together on setting boundaries that are comfortable for both of you.

> *In late recovery, the courage it takes to get the*
> *help and healing you need is the greatest gift you*
> *can give to yourself and to your partner.*

The Benefits of Late Recovery

The rewards of working through all of these late-recovery problems extend far past the relationships themselves. The reason you seek out partners who trigger your issues is that those issues need to be healed. You need healing for your peace of mind; for your mental, emotional, and spiritual growth; and for the safety of your recovery. Relapse over unhealed childhood issues is not uncommon in late recovery. Afraid of facing these problems, many people drift into unhealthy ways of thinking, managing feelings, and acting. Eventually, relapse seems like the only way out.

In this stage, the courage it takes to get the help and healing you need is the greatest gift you can give to yourself and to your partner. Your relationship might not survive the process, but if you don't do the work, your relationship will fail anyway. And if you go through the healing process together, as true friends instead of enemies, your love will be graced with a depth and a commitment you've never known before.

Thought and Discussion Questions

1. What are three ways a committed romantic partnership can help your sobriety?
2. What are three ways a committed romantic partnership can get in the way of your sobriety?
3. What is one main thing you need in a committed romantic partnership?
4. What is one main thing you fear in a committed romantic partnership?
5. What is one behavior you consider unforgivable in a committed romantic partnership?
6. How will you know when you're ready for a committed romantic partnership?
7. How will you know if you're not ready for a committed romantic partnership?

Chapter 10

Maintenance

When the trials of late recovery are over, do you float off into some heaven on earth, where relationships are blissful and single time unfolds like a flower? Of course not. You're human, so you keep making mistakes, losing your way, and getting stuck from time to time. But you have a number of tools to correct your mistakes, find your way, and get unstuck as quickly as possible. Time and experience have taught you that healthy recovery is the easier, softer way.

> **In this chapter, you'll be looking at:**
> * Relationship recovery tasks in the maintenance stage
> * Relationship-related stuck points
> * Healthy relationships

Nick has eighteen years' sobriety, but he wouldn't think about trying to make it without his support system. The crazy stage that he went through in late recovery was enough to convince him that he still needs input from other recovering people. He likes himself, but the memory of all the years of hurting himself is still fresh in his mind. The tenth through twelfth steps (daily self-inventory, spiritual growth, and carrying the message) are important to Nick on a daily basis. When he's been wrong, when he's spouted off to his fiancée, he knows he has the tenth step (daily and spot-check inventory) as a way of correcting his mistakes quickly and cleanly. Through the eleventh step (spiritual growth) he keeps his sense of wonder, joy, and purpose alive. And his twelfth step work (carrying the message to others) refreshes his life and does as much for him as it does for the people he helps.

Nick still goes to meetings, but he's also expanded his efforts at personal growth and change. He takes classes as often as his work will let him, and he pursues his spiritual interests. He works hard to stay physically healthy and spends high-quality time with his fiancée. His life is full and balanced. He has plenty of problems, but he works on them until they're solved. He no longer runs away from life or tries to beat it into submission.

Relationship-related stuck points can include:

- The return of post-acute withdrawal symptoms
- Fear of intimacy
- Fear of being worthless or not good enough
- Fear of being vulnerable to another human being
- Fear of being trapped or abandoned

Relationship Recovery Tasks in the Maintenance Stage

In maintenance, you incorporate recovery principles into all aspects of your life. You get on with life: building relationships, families, and careers. Your life is no longer focused on alcohol or drugs, on primary recovery from those substances, or on the healing of childhood wounds. For that reason, if you're going to be in a relationship, you need someone who will continue to support you in your recovery but also have something to offer you in your life beyond the recovery stages. Your relationship must be healthy, and you must be able to build recovery into the process. That way you can remember where you came from, so you'll never have to go back again.

> **Relationship recovery tasks in maintenance:**
>
> - Get on with life—building relationships, families, and careers.
> - Find partners who will continue to support you in your recovery and your full life.
> - Develop healthy relationships.
> - Build recovery into the process.

Relationship-Related Stuck Points

At any stage of recovery it's possible to fall back into old problems and behavior patterns. Issues that belong more appropriately to another stage can come up even after many years' sobriety. Under high stress, it's possible to have the symptoms of post-acute withdrawal return (difficulty thinking clearly, managing feelings, avoiding accidents, managing stress, remembering things, or sleeping restfully), even in the maintenance stage. Fortunately, you have all the tools you've built up during the first five stages of recovery. Those tools work well, but only if you use them.

Some of the most common relationship stuck points involve concepts that have been introduced in earlier chapters: fear of intimacy, fear of being worthless or not good enough, fear of becoming vulnerable to another human being, and fear of being trapped or abandoned. In maintenance it's easy to fall into the trap of saying you "shouldn't" be having these problems at this point in your recovery. That in itself can be an excuse not to find and accept the help you need.

Payoffs for Stuck Points

There are some payoffs for staying stuck. One is that it's comfortable; it's familiar. Being stuck is an excuse not to try, not to risk failure. It's an excuse not to change. It's an excuse not to put in a lot of effort. And it's very, very common. Many people, in and out of recovery, spend more time stuck than unstuck. Getting unstuck requires courage and effort.

Responses to Stuck Points

Many people respond to stuck points by sinking into addictive behavior: overeating, compulsive working, compulsive exercise, cheating on their partners, etc. They run away from the discomfort of being stuck, instead of working through the stuck point. These substitute compulsions may feel good at the moment, but they cause problems that feel worse later. They don't solve the problems, and they cause new problems.

Some common payoffs for stuck points:
- Being stuck can be comfortable and familiar.
- It's an excuse not to try, and not to risk failure.
- It's an excuse not to change.
- It's an excuse not to put in a lot of effort.

Martha used to cope with her relationship problems by throwing herself into her work and staying away from her partner as much as possible. That only made the problems worse, and it drove her employees crazy. She finally admitted that, after all the growth and recovery she'd been through, she still needed help with her relationship. Her partner was more than willing to work with her, once she stopped running away.

They made an appointment for a refresher session with their former counselor. But before they kept that appointment, they spent a day walking together in the woods, not talking about their problems—not talking about much of anything—just getting away from it all together. When they came back into the real world, they felt refreshed. They were much more clear-headed and better able to straighten out their problems than they would have been if they'd tried to tackle these issues a couple of days earlier. They detached from the problem and so gained a better perspective on it.

Thought and Discussion Questions

1. When you get any symptoms of post-acute withdrawal (difficulty thinking clearly, managing feelings, avoiding accidents, managing stress, remembering things, or sleeping restfully), what do you do to cope with those symptoms?
2. What might be some more effective ways of coping with those symptoms?
3. In your relationships, do you still experience fears of intimacy or of being worthless, vulnerable, trapped, or abandoned? When do you tend to feel these kinds of fears?
4. What are your personal payoffs for staying stuck?
5. What are the penalties for staying stuck?
6. What are three productive ways of managing stuck points in your relationships?
7. What are two ways you can get objective feedback and work on solutions to your relationship problems?

Are Healthy Relationships Boring?

Most of us grew up on televised images of stormy relationships whose passion was based on conflict. If the wounds are healed and the conflict settles down, will we lose the passion and the excitement? "Oh, it's not boring," said Jeannette. "Anytime you have the courage to open up and be honest about something your partner doesn't want to hear, that's a risk. Anytime you have the courage to really be there for someone when he's at his most vulnerable, you're both taking a risk. True intimacy is still a little bit scary."

The twelfth step (carrying the message) says that we tried to "practice these principles in all our affairs." At any stage of recovery, intimate relationships are the most difficult field for practicing the principles of healthy recovery. Even after the bulk of

195

your late-recovery issues have been healed, you'll still have "buttons," and your partner will sometimes push them. "He still triggers me, and I trigger him," Jeannette said of her longtime partner. "Only now instead of taking a few hours to realize what's going on and work through it, it takes us about five minutes." That's progress that you can live with.

> *At any stage of recovery, intimate relationships*
> *are the most difficult field for practicing the*
> *principles of healthy recovery.*

One of the benefits of healthy relationships is that they don't take up as much thought or energy as troubled relationships. You're both free to live full lives, together and as individuals. Monica has a new business, a volunteer position, five nieces, and three people she sponsors. Don has a demanding job, two children from a former marriage, Spanish lessons, and five people he sponsors. Together they're learning ballroom dancing. They never run out of things to do or talk about. Most of the drama in their lives comes from other people's lives, and they prefer it that way.

Drama hurts too much. Peace feels good. They're willing to work on themselves and on their relationship to cultivate that peace, protect it, and watch it grow.

Appendix
The Twelve Steps

The twelve steps you're about to read were developed in Alcoholics Anonymous (AA) and later adopted (with slight wording changes) by other 12-Step recovery groups. The explanations of these steps were taken from the book *Understanding the Twelve Steps: A Guide for Counselors, Therapists, and Recovering People* by Terence T. Gorski (Independence, Missouri: Herald House/Independence Press, 1989). These explanations can give you a beginning understanding of how to "work" the steps—use them to get and stay sober. Twelve-Step group members, and the literature of those programs, can give you more information.

These steps haven't worked for everyone, but they've helped millions of people achieve lasting recovery. Twelve-Step groups like Alcoholics Anonymous, Narcotics Anonymous, Cocaine Anonymous, Al-Anon, and Alateen are listed in the telephone directories in all major United States cities, and in many smaller communities as well.

Step One: **We admitted we were powerless over alcohol— that our lives had become unmanageable.**

In the first step, you admit that you can't control your drinking or drug use and that, because of that powerlessness, your life is out of control. The first step is designed to help alcoholics and addicts grasp a basic and undeniable fact: Whenever you use alcohol (or other drugs), you can never be sure what is going to happen. This is the essence of being out of control. Sometimes alcoholics drink in moderation with no harmful effects. At other times, without any rhyme or reason, their drinking escalates and they act out in ways that hurt both themselves and those they love.

The key to working a first step is to recognize that you have a problem, then acknowledge that you've tried everything you know to solve the problem and none of it worked. In essence, you honestly acknowledge that you can't solve the problem by doing the things you have learned how to do. In short, "You can't do it alone."

Step Two: Came to believe that a Power greater than ourselves could restore us to sanity.

In step two, you become open to the possibility that there is someone or something out there that is able to provide a way to help you solve your problems. This step asks you to believe that someone or something more powerful—smarter, stronger, and more knowledgeable than you—can help you stop drinking or drugging.

At the core of the second step is the belief in some kind of Higher Power that can help you. You need to believe you can tap into a source of courage, strength, and hope that will allow you to cope. After completing the second step, you can say with complete honesty, "We can't, but somebody else can." You don't have to know what or who that Higher Power is; you just have to believe that it exists and become willing to search for it.

Step Three: Made a decision to turn our will and our lives over to the care of God *as we understood Him*.

Step three tells recovering people to trust in a Higher Power. In other words, find some expert advice and follow it. They must be willing to take directions from their newfound Higher Power and see what happens. But who or what is that Higher Power? AA states very clearly that it is up to you to find your own Higher Power. Notice that the terms "Higher Power" and "God" are used interchangeably. AA doesn't prescribe a specific concept of God, but rather instructs its members to find a God of their own understanding.

You can select God as your Higher Power, but many members, especially new members, don't. They use their 12-Step group as their first Higher Power. The group meets all of the criteria. By going to meetings and talking honestly with group members, you can tap into a strong belief that recovery is possible. You can develop the courage, strength, and hope to go on. By listening to the stories of your group members, you can learn what to do in order to get well. As you work at your recovery, you can share your progress and problems with other people who will listen to you, understand your struggles, and take seriously what you're saying.

Step Four: **Made a searching and fearless moral inventory of ourselves.**

After working the first three steps, you're "into" the program. You're willing to accept and follow advice. The first definitive piece of advice you receive is in step four, which tells you to examine yourself critically to find out who you really are. You need to look within and take an inventory of your strengths and weaknesses, so you can build on your strengths and overcome your weaknesses.

It's only through an honest knowledge of yourself and your motivations that you can find long-term sobriety. You must be willing to challenge the misperceptions and mistaken beliefs that you hold. Even if it hurts, you must get to know who you really are in both your strengths and your weaknesses. This rigorous honesty forms the foundation of recovery.

Step Five: **Admitted to God, to ourselves, and to another human being the exact nature of our wrongs.**

In step five, you need to admit both your addiction and the character defects you found in step four that drive you back into your old addictive ways of coping. You're instructed to (1) admit to yourself, (2) affirm with your Higher Power, and (3) share with another person, as honestly as you can, your inventory of your strengths and weaknesses. This inventory is not a litany of sins but rather an honest evaluation of what you've learned about yourself and your self-defeating behaviors.

In AA, this is humility. And it doesn't mean you put yourself down. Humility means you know who you are, know where you're coming from, and accept that it's OK for you to have your particular strengths and weaknesses.

It's only by confronting yourself in a dialogue with another human being that you can truly come to terms with what has happened to you and what you've become as a result of your addictive experiences. Sharing painful past memories with a caring person—one who will understand what you're saying, take you seriously, and affirm your experiences as real and valid—provides a sense of relief. You no longer feel alone. You no longer feel like an outcast. You realize that others have done things similar to what you've done. You can see that you belong and you can recover.

Step Six: **Were entirely ready to have God remove all these defects of character.**

By working step six, you live with a conscious awareness of the character defects you discovered in steps four and five. By being constantly aware of your character defects and the pain they are causing you and those you love, you become ready and willing to give them up. You keep asking for the courage, the strength, and the means to correct them.

Step Seven: **Humbly asked Him to remove our shortcomings.**

In step seven, you ask your Higher Power to remove your shortcomings. You ask for the strength to do what you need to do to change and grow and leave your addictive self behind. Your Higher Power gives you the courage and strength to give up your character defects, but you must do the actual giving up. You must take action and do what AA calls the "legwork." AA literature constantly points out this dual role—turning to a Higher Power for courage, strength, and hope, and then putting this newfound strength into action.

Step Eight: **Made a list of all persons we had harmed, and became willing to make amends to them all.**

In step eight, you come to the realization that your past addictive behavior damaged other people. You make a list of those people and recognize that you must make an honest attempt to repair the hurt you did to them. In other words, you acknowledge that you must make amends.

Step Nine: **Made direct amends to such people wherever possible, except when to do so would injure them or others.**

You make amends to all you have harmed. You actually repair any damage you have caused, wherever or whenever it's in your power to do so. You "clean house" and make room for spiritual growth.

Step Ten: **Continued to take personal inventory and when we were wrong promptly admitted it.**

You take inventory of yourself daily, examining your thoughts, feelings, and actions. When you goof, when you create a problem, when you prove you're a fallible human being, you fix the problems as quickly and honestly as you can, and to the best of your abilities. This frees you to make your primary focus that of spiritual growth in your recovery.

Step Eleven: **Sought through prayer and meditation to improve our conscious contact with God** *as we understood Him*, **praying only for knowledge of His will for us and the power to carry that out.**

When you were practicing your addiction, alcohol and drugs distorted your spiritual values. The term "spiritual" means the nonphysical aspect of your being—your thoughts, feelings, attitudes, and values. As you clear the wreckage from the past, you can at last experience a new sense of spiritual freedom. You can contact the psychic energy or life-force within you in new and exciting ways. You can learn to become still and listen to that quiet, yet powerful voice within you that connects you to your true values in life. In AA terms, you can develop conscious contact with the God of your understanding—your Higher Power.

Step Twelve: **Having had a spiritual awakening as the result of these steps, we tried to carry this message to alcoholics, and to practice these principles in all our affairs.**

What AA calls a "spiritual awakening" is a radical transformation or change in perception, attitude, and personality. You begin to feel changed because you're thinking differently, managing your feelings differently, and acting differently. You've changed in subtle yet profound ways. Because of these changes, you're ready to go out and carry the message of what you've learned and experienced to other recovering people. It's important to remember that step twelve also instructs you to keep practicing 12-Step principles in all of your affairs. Thus, working the 12-Step program never ends.